Christmas Thoughts

2010

By Dr. Delron Shirley

Cover design by Konya Ferrell

Dedication

To my sons Jonathan, Christopher, and Jeremy.
It is in children that we most easily discover
the true thoughts of Christmas.

Table of Contents

Slow as Christmas

When I was a child, we used the expression "slow as Christmas" to describe things that seemed a long time in coming. For certain, the coming of God's plan of redemption into the world seemed as slow as Christmas.

God had promised the messiah immediately after Adam and Eve had sinned. Certainly, that offer of a seed from the woman to crush the head of the seed of the serpent gladdened the hearts of the father and mother of the human race. It is likely that they expected its fulfillment in Cain or Abel. However, when the jealousy of one of the brothers left one dead and the other stained with the sin of murder, their hopes of the messiah were dashed. When Seth -- whose very name indicates that he was a substitute and, hopefully, a replacement in the quest for a redeemer -- did not prove to be a savior, Adam and Eve must have questioned the slowness of Christmas.

Eventually, the citizens of Planet Earth became so evil and all their thoughts were so polluted that Jehovah decided to destroy the whole lot. However, there was one singular character who stood out against the background of depraved humanity -- the righteous Noah. Was this man the promised messiah, the anticipated seed? No, he also proved to be human and fallible. Again, we question the slowness of Christmas.

Eventually, God chose one man named Abram and called him from paganism to become His chosen representative among men. Renamed Abraham, meaning "father of nations," this patriarch waited and waited and waited for God to make good to him the promise of an appointed seed as a covenant heir. Year after year sifted through the hourglass of time as

Abraham wondered if Christmas would ever come. Finally, the barrenness of Sarah's womb and Abraham's impotence gave way to the miracle child Isaac. Even this long-awaited son was not the promised seed of the woman; Christmas still had not come!

Isaac's sons Jacob and Esau became our next candidates for the promised seed, but they as well proved inadequate contenders through Esau's careless disregard for God's covenant blessing and birthright and Jacob's cheating and greed. Jacob eventually had a divine encounter which renewed mankind's hopes that he might produce the anticipated seed. Yet, his marriages were riddled with conflict and barrenness, delaying the longed-for Christmas. At last, Joseph -- the son of his old age -- seemed to be in the running as our Christmas herald. Envy and sibling rivalry doomed this young dreamer to a life of slavery and prison. Even though God supernaturally delivered him from the dungeon and set him on the throne of the greatest world empire of that day, Joseph still fell far short of the messianic expectations. Christmas was still slow in coming!

It was four hundred years before even another glimmer of hope danced on the horizon of human anticipation. A talking bush, a rod that became a snake and then a rod again, ten plagues, and a sea that transformed into a highway proved the authenticity of the divine appointment upon the life of the boy who was drawn out of the bulrushes. Even though Moses led the people of God out of human bondage, he could not free them from the slavery of demonic dominion. Deliverance seemed as slow as Christmas.

As little children mark the days and adults frantically count down the shopping days to Christmas, the human race must have longed to pull the pages from the calendar of destiny as the centuries crept by at a snail's pace. A few promising individuals blazed out against the dark sky of human desperation, yet these bright stars soon lost their sparkle. King David fell subject to adultery and murder. King Solomon yielded to every form of excess. The whole family of God's people failed so miserably that God abandoned them to seventy long years of slavery and captivity among the Babylonians.

Almost to the point of giving up on the promise, the human family was awakened one clear night by the sound of angels and the light of a brilliant star announcing that the four-millennia wait had finally come to its fruition. Slow as it had been, Christmas had finally come! Jesus was born in Bethlehem. The fulfillment of all the dreams and hopes of earth and the curiosity of heaven had finally come. "For verily I say unto you, that many prophets and righteous men have desired to see those things which ye see, and have not seen them; and to hear those things which ye hear, and have not heard them." (Matthew 13:17) "Unto whom it was revealed, that not unto themselves, but unto us they did minister the things, which are now reported unto you by them that have preached the gospel unto you with the Holy Ghost sent down from heaven; which things the angels desire to look into." (I Peter 1:12)

The desire of all nations had come. "And I will shake all nations, and the desire of all nations shall come: and I will fill this house with glory, saith the LORD of hosts." (Haggai 2:7)

Christmas had finally come!

The Perfect Gift

   A famous line from Louisa Mae Alcott's classic Little Women sums up much of what we feel about this holiday season, "Christmas won't be Christmas without any presents." How much time, energy, and money we invest in picking just the right gifts for all our friends and relatives. How many times do we go back and forth to the sales counter to look at, pick up, put down, reconsider, buy, return, and maybe even buy again that gift which doesn't seem just right for that hard-to-buy-for person on our gift list? My wife even sometimes buys two gifts and takes them home to decide, intending to return one of the gifts.
   Sometimes the gift buying and giving -- not to mention the gift receiving -- seems to eclipse the real meaning of the season. However, when gifts are exchanged from the right attitude of the heart, they enhance and establish the spirit of Christmas. O'Henry, in The Gift of the Magi, spins a tale of a young couple who wanted to give the perfect gift to each other. Jim's treasured possession was a family heirloom, a magnificent pocket watch, so Della determined to buy him a beautiful chain suitable for the exquisite antique. The bride's glory was her long, splendid hair, and Jim was set on purchasing jeweled hair combs to adorn her fabulous locks. Each found a way to fulfill these dreams even though the gifts far exceeded their meager budgets. What joy awaited these lovers as they opened their gifts on Christmas morning. Della could hardly contain herself waiting to see the watch attached to the new chain she had purchased. Jim was equally eager to see displayed in his wife's strands the combs he had sacrificed so dearly to purchase. Alas, the twist of the story is that

4

Della had sold her hair to the wig maker in order to buy the watch chain and Jim had pawned his watch for the combs! The true gifts came not in the boxes and bows, but in the sacrifice that filled the boxes and love that tied the bows!

The best Christmas story of all is set half a world away from the snowy scenes we associate with our white Christmases. It came not in December and not in the warm hearth-side setting of a tree surrounded with mounds of brightly wrapped packages. This story came from the horrors of the Vietnam War. A mortar round had crashed into a mission orphanage, killing the missionaries and some of the children. When an American Navy doctor and nurse arrived, they found one critically injured eight-year-old girl. She needed a transfusion immediately. The results of quick tests showed that one of the uninjured children had a matching blood type. When the medical team asked the boy to give his blood to save his friend's life, he responded at first with wide-eyed silence. In her limited French, the nurse explained to Heng what they were going to do. The young boy then lay down and prepared to give his blood. As the transfusion began, he burst into uncontrollable sobs. By this time, a Vietnamese nurse had arrived and began to try to console Heng. She explained to the Americans that the young boy had expected to die. He had thought that the doctor was going to take all of his blood in order to save the little girl's life. Heng explained in just one short sentence why he was willing to volunteer for the transfusion even though he thought it meant giving his life, "She's my friend." These three words remind us of the biblical explanation of Christmas, "Greater love hath no man than this, that a man lay down his life for his friends." (John 15:13) Yet the Bible goes much further in explaining why Christ came. Paul, in Romans 5:10, tells us that it was more than our friendship that caused Jesus to give His blood for us. "For if, when we were enemies, we were reconciled to God by the death of his Son, much more, being reconciled, we shall be saved by his life."

The true story of Christmas is told only in the story of Easter. In Bethlehem, God gave His son and the wise men gave their gold, frankincense, and myrrh; but at Calvary, Jesus gave His all. He gave on the cosmic level what Heng was willing to give in that little bombed-out orphanage in Vietnam. In fact, we know that the whole purpose of Christmas was to make Good Friday and Easter possible. One artist portrayed the life of Christ in a most dramatic series of paintings. The first was the nativity scene with the Bethlehem star shining brightly outside the stable door. As the shafts of light from the star fell on the manger, a couple of the rafters blotted out the light to cast a cross-like shadow across the Christ child. The second of the paintings was of Jesus as a toddler running to the waiting arms of His mother. With the sun behind Mary, her outstretched arms formed another cross-shaped shadow across the path of her young son. Next in the series is Jesus as a teenager working at Joseph's carpenter's bench. The sun's rays passing through the supply of wood randomly stacked in the father's shop again formed the shadow of the cross upon the adolescent. Jesus' whole destiny was bound to one act of giving -- the giving of His life on Golgotha's hill. This was the perfect Christmas gift. "And I, if I be lifted up from the earth, will draw all men unto me." (John 12:32)

The Apostle Paul spoke of Jesus' Christmas gift to us in II Corinthians 9:15, "Thanks be unto God for his unspeakable gift." As Jim and Della must have been left speechless when they realized the sacrifices each had made; and, as those doctors and nurses at the little orphanage must have been dumbfounded by Heng's heroic act of selflessness -- we find ourselves unable to adequately express that gift of God's love in Jesus' appearance on Planet Earth.

The Psalmist David caught a glimpse of that unspeakable gift and described it prophetically some thousand years before the event. In Psalm 22 he masterfully spreads out the canvas and sketches out the entire scene of Calvary.

My God, my God, why hast thou forsaken me? why art thou so far from helping me, and from the words of my roaring? O my God, I cry in the daytime, but thou hearest not; and in the night season, and am not silent. But thou art holy, O thou that inhabitest the praises of Israel. Our fathers trusted in thee: they trusted, and thou didst deliver them. They cried unto thee, and were delivered: they trusted in thee, and were not confounded. But I am a worm, and no man; a reproach of men, and despised of the people. All they that see me laugh me to scorn: they shoot out the lip, they shake the head saying, He trusted on the LORD that he would deliver him: let him deliver him, seeing he delighted in him. But thou art he that took me out of the womb: thou didst make me hope when I was upon my mother's breasts. I was cast upon thee from the womb: thou art my God from my mother's belly. Be not far from me; for trouble is near; for there is none to help. Many bulls have compassed me: strong bulls of Bashan have beset me round. They gaped upon me with their mouths, as a ravening and a roaring lion. I am poured out like water, and all my bones are out of joint: my heart is like wax; it is melted in the midst of my bowels. My strength is dried up like a potsherd; and my tongue cleaveth to my jaws; and thou hast brought me into the dust of death. For dogs have compassed me: the assembly of the wicked have enclosed me: they pierced my hands and my feet. I may tell all my bones: they look and stare upon me. They part my garments among them, and cast lots upon my vesture. But be not thou far from me, O LORD: O my strength, haste thee to help me. Deliver my soul from the sword; my darling from the power of the dog. Save me from the lion's mouth: for thou hast heard me from the horns of the unicorns. I will declare thy name unto my brethren: in the midst of the congregation will I praise thee.

Perhaps this revelation of the unspeakable gift that God was giving to mankind was on David's mind and in his heart when he was offered the sacrifice spot on Temple Mount as a free gift. If so, then we can readily understand why he responded, "Neither will I offer burnt offerings unto the LORD my God of that which doth cost me nothing." (II Samuel 24:24)

This Christmas season, let's not only pick the right gifts for all our friends and relatives, let's find the right gift for the One who gave us the unspeakable gift -- Himself and His life; let's give to Jesus ourselves and our lives.

Wise Men -- A Christmas Key

The wise men seem out of place in the Gospel of Matthew. If this volume is -- as most Bible students say -- written for the Jewish people to read, why did Matthew include this story of gentile astrologers at the nativity? Why did he not relate to us the story of the nice Jewish shepherds who also visited the new-born messiah? On the surface, it seems totally out of line that these gentiles would play such an important role in the story of the Jewish messiah. It is almost unthinkable that these magi -- soothsayers, magicians, and astrologers -- should be considered in this Jewish gospel since the Jewish faith considered such demon-inspired men as abominations to God. (Deuteronomy 18:10-14)

But here they are, bigger than life, following a mysterious star which led them to the messiah. Many scholars through history have pondered the essence of that star of Bethlehem. Some have suggested that it was a nova, an exploding star. Most have rejected that idea since a nova would have been seen and noted by all the ancient people. Herod, however, had to ask the men when the star had appeared -- indicating that it was not something that had been notable in the skies of Israel. Other scholars have suggested that this star was a comet; however, this idea has been soundly rejected since comets throughout history, in almost all cultures, have been considered bad omens. A comet would have been considered an announcement of the death of a king, not the birth of a new one. After searching all of the resources of astronomy, many scholars have settled upon the idea that the star the wise men saw was something that only a skilled student of the heavens would notice -- a conjunction of the planets. Just before the birth of Jesus, there was a rare triple conjunction of Jupiter and Saturn in the area of Pisces which astrologers considered to signify Israel. This same conjunction had occurred three years prior to the birth of Moses who delivered Israel from Egypt. Could it be that its reoccurrence foretold the birth of another great deliverer in Israel? It is interesting to note here that Herod's response after his investigation with the wise men was to kill all the children who were two years old and younger -- an amazing correlation with the reaction of Pharaoh when the star appeared in Egypt.

The more we see of the wise men, the greater the enigma becomes. Why are these gentiles who practice an abominable religion and star gazing introduced in this Jewish gospel? Perhaps the very fact that they are called "wise men" holds a key. In the book of Daniel, we find several confrontations between the Hebrews and the astrologers of Babylon. From the beginning, Daniel and his friends prove to be ten times wiser than the wise men of Babylon. On several occasions, Daniel is pitted against these astrologers and always comes out ahead. In each confrontation, he shows his colors and wins "hands down." The wisdom of Solomon set him far ahead of the thinkers of all his surrounding nations. His book of Proverbs exalts the precious qualities of wisdom. Perhaps the appearance of the wise men (soothsayers, magicians) was to bring the Jewish people back to their foundational concept that they, not the gentile nations, were to be the wise ones on Planet Earth.

> Behold, I have taught you statutes and
> judgments, even as the LORD my God
> commanded me, that ye should do so
> in the land whither ye go to possess it.

Keep therefore and do them; for this is your wisdom and your understanding in the sight of the nations, which shall hear all these statutes, and say, Surely this great nation is a wise and understanding people. For what nation is there so great, who hath God so nigh unto them, as the LORD our God is in all things that we call upon Him for? And what nation is there so great that hath statutes and judgments so righteous as all this law, which I set before you this day? (Deuteronomy 4:5-8)

All other nations who did not recognize Jehovah were fools. "The fool hath said in his heart, There is no God. They are corrupt, they have done abominable works, there is none that doeth good." (Psalms 14:1)

It was only in beginning to acknowledge and reverence the one true God that anyone could obtain wisdom. "The fear of the LORD is the beginning of wisdom: and the knowledge of the holy is understanding." (Proverbs 9:10)

With this thought in mind, the story of these out-of-place magi suddenly takes on new meaning. Perhaps these strangers are not so out-of-place after all. In fact, their visit actually sets the stage and determines the tone of the whole book. This gospel becomes a commentary on who is a wise man and who is a foolish man.

A Jew Looks at Jesus

I am writing the next few pages from the inside of a Jewish reader's mind as he struggles through the book of Matthew -- a book which attracts and repels him at the same time. Certain obvious license has been taken to make the text more reader friendly for a modern American audience. For example, our national holidays have been substituted for the Jewish counterparts. However, every attempt has been made to keep the ideas and reactions within context. Let's join our host as he questions, "Who are the wise men and who are the fools?"

"King Herod, there are men here to see you. They say they have come from a distant land to see the child that is born king of the Jews." These words shook Herod to his very soul and he didn't know whether to laugh or cry, to fight or run. Through his mind flashed the whole drama of his rise to the Judean throne. "King of the Jews -- why, I am the king of the Jews. Ha, I'm the first real king the Jews have had since the Roman takeover. Those others before me -- why, they were little more than dukes. The Romans held a tight reign on everything they did. But I, with my political pull and a few pay-offs, won for myself the title 'king of Judea.' Yeah, it took a little while to gain the kingdom that went with that title; but, I soon won the political power away from the Sadducees and aristocrats who seem to have all the angles figured out. A little blood here, some money there, and the right choice for a wife -- how could I lose? Even after I gained the throne, there were a few little family matters I had to straighten out to keep my own family from robbing my throne. Now here are these strangers from some mystic country in the East claiming that the stars are prophesying against my throne. Men I can execute, but stars are beyond my reach!"

Reluctantly, he gives the word for these strangers to enter and the interrogation begins:

"From where have you come?"

"From a distant land in the East."

"And exactly what is your interest in Judea?"

"Your Highness, we are astrologers. We are responsible in our kingdom for watching the stars and learning their secrets. You see, we believe that they hold the plans for the nations. We recognize the stars, especially the wandering stars, as gods. How they move in the sky reveals their intentions for the nations. We have built great towers so that we can approach the sky, and we have dug deep pits so that we can see the stars even when the sun is shining. Several months ago, while we were watching from our great ziggurat tower, we saw the stars crossing and re-crossing in the heavens. Our charts, legends, and logs of star movements did not record that such an event had happened since many centuries ago. We knew that some great event was about to occur but we had only one clue to the interpretation of that event. The position in the sky and the place of the constellations indicated that the stars spoke of the Jews. Hungry for an explanation we searched among the scrolls of your prophets which have been preserved in our country since the time that the Jewish people were enslaved there and your prophet Daniel served in high positions among our wise men. There, in the words of a gentile prophet whose words are recorded in your Hebrew scripture, we found our answer! The book of Numbers records Balaam's prophecy, 'I see him but not now; I behold him, but not nigh: A star shall come forth out of Jacob, and a scepter shall rise out of Israel.' Immediately, we took leave of our positions and came to see the one who shall soon hold the scepter of Israel. The star we have seen and the new king we also desire to see!"

"And what are your intentions once you see this

new king?"

"We have come to show him honor. We have gifts from our land -- gifts befitting a king. We want to worship him and to confirm the message we have received from the stars."

"Well, I know nothing about this new king -- but I, too, have a surprise for him and would like to see him. Let me call in the scribes and chief priests to find out more about these prophecies."

From that first scene, the story begins to unfold. It's a most intriguing story -- a combination of adventure, love, tragedy, mystery, surprise, and victory -- a story of divine intervention in human affairs. It begins in the halls of a royal palace with an intrusion by mysterious astrologers and soothsayers from a land of demon worshipers and weaves its way to a political execution at the city dump where there is again an unexpected intrusion. The surprise ending exceeds even the talents of O'Henry. It's the story of the true king of the Jews as recorded by Matthew, one of the first to proclaim himself a subject of this king. Matthew tries to explain why he has and why others should become subjects of this Jesus, king of the Jews.

Son of David, Son of Abraham

He titles his book with a rather long but intriguing caption, "The book of the generation of Jesus Christ, the son of David, the son of Abraham." As usual, the title is a clue to Matthew's intentions for his work. Matthew is proclaiming that Jesus is the son of David and the son of Abraham. He does not see Jesus as a son of David and of Abraham, but the son of David and of Abraham. To Matthew, Jesus is the unique son who stands as the covenant recipient of both the Abrahamic and Davidic covenants. That means that Jesus is the messiah and a true Jew. These are key points in the controversy concerning Jesus, who is probably the most controversial person to have ever arisen in Jewish circles. The high priest called His doctrine heresy, and the government executed Him as a political criminal; yet His controversy continues to rage. His followers claim that He rose from the dead and is still alive.

Even now there are more followers than ever and the synagogues throughout the Jewish world still question this heretic from Galilee. There is one good turn of events -- more and more Gentiles are joining the movement of this self-styled prophet. Is it possible that someday the Jews will be completely rid of this Jesus religion? Will only uncircumcised Gentiles be its followers? In the meantime, many Jews are reading Matthew's book to help understand this other religion. That title either repels them or intrigues them. Matthew pulls no punches. There is no mistake that he insists that Jesus really is the messiah and a true Jew -- the heir to God's covenants through Abraham and David.

"Son of David" is the most popular title used among Jews to speak of the messiah. It was David who gathered the twelve loose tribes into one strong nation. It was David who established Jerusalem as the political and spiritual capital of the nation. It was David who defeated the enemies of Israel and collected their wealth for Israel's treasury. It was David who called all the tribes together to become one nation under his leadership and the rule of God. Immediately after David, the nation began to break up. Solomon strained the loyalties of his subjects and plowed the ground for anarchy. Following him, Rehoboam and Jeroboam finished the job. Israel was no longer one nation but two. Suddenly, the glory of Israel was only a memory -- and a hope. In the heart of every true Israelite there burned -- and still burns -- a spark of hope that a new David will arise and again reunite the nation. The prophets promise that a new king will arise out of David and that his throne will never end. The rabbis use the term "son of David" to speak of their long-awaited messiah. Of the many titles for the messiah, none other gained the place in the hearts of the people as did "Son of David." On the lips of the common people, in the pages of the Talmud, in the hope of the hearts of Israel's leaders -- "son of David" is a word of encouragement that sparks a fire of joy and faith. No Jew can read Matthew's connection of Jesus with the Son of David without being stirred to hope -- or to anger! It is an unthinkably bold claim to call a crucified political criminal the messiah of Israel!

Matthew ties Jesus with the Jews by using the standard Jewish title, "son of Abraham." Unlike Luke who traces Jesus' genealogy back to Adam, Matthew stops at Abraham in uprooting Jesus' family tree. Is Luke trying to let all men experience a relationship to Jesus while Matthew is aiming at letting the Jews feel that kinship? Perhaps many of the Jews would rather push Jesus off on the Gentiles -- but Matthew is saying, "No, he's a Jew -- and a kosher Jew at that! Even more, he is the unique recipient of Abraham's blessing."

Matthew begins his book with the page of "begat"s. It's enough to make any sensible person put down the book and not worry with such boring style. On the other hand, those readers who have been made curious by the book's opening sentence are compelled to find out why this Jesus can be called the son of David and the son of Abraham. Since the "begat"s prove Him to be at least a physical descendent of David and of Abraham, they are not such boring reading after all. However, the genealogies really come alive with verse seventeen. Here Matthew points out that all of Jewish history seems to be bracketed off in sections of fourteen generations. Every fourteen generations, Israel reaches a turning point in her history: Abraham, David, the Babylonian exile, and now Jesus! Jesus seems to be equated with Abraham, David, and the Exile! The number fourteen is in itself a bit of a mathematical puzzle -- it's the sum of the numerical values of the Hebrew letters in David's name. Using only the consonants, as traditional Hebrew does, the D is the fourth letter in the alphabet and the V is the sixth. Thus DVD represents 4+6+4 which sums to 14. Is Matthew saying that Jesus is not only a physical descendant but also a spiritual descendant of David? Is Jesus the long-awaited son of David?

Wise Men and Fools

Well, back to the plot. In Herod's palace, the audience with the magi is in session. He has called in the scribes and the chief priests to inquire about the prophecies concerning the king of the Jews. With a unanimous decision, the scholars proclaim that the messiah is to be born in Bethlehem. The prophet Micah had predicted it that way. As the magi inquire concerning directions to Bethlehem, the scribes and priests dismiss themselves from the king's court. Here, Matthew begins to give the readers a taste of the book's theme. He has introduced two groups of radically different people. One is the scribes and priests of Israel. They spend their lives studying the scrolls of the law and prophets hoping to find the wisdom of God. They can recite word-for-word whole books of the Hebrew scripture. In addition, they know verbatim the expositions and arguments of the great rabbis. Their arm bands and head bands are inscribed with portions of the Torah, their law. Hours each day are spent in study and memorization of Torah. Prayers and religious ritual are constantly their way of life. The coming messiah is the hope of their existence -- the climax for which the whole drama of life awaits. On the other hand is the group of magi. Being gentiles, they are outside the covenant and promises of God. Uncircumcised and eating defiled meat, they worship the stars and practice all forms of magic condemned by the Hebrew scripture. Strangely, it is these unworthy pagans to whom the messiah is revealed. Even when the holy men of Israel are let in on the news, they are not happy or even curious over the possibility that their messiah has come. Alone, the magi set out for Bethlehem, while the scribes and priests wind through the crooked streets of Jerusalem. In their own little homes, their lives continue as if nothing has happened, while only a few miles away lies the fulfillment of all their hopes. How great a paradox it is that the Jewish rabbis traditionally refer to one another as "wise ones," but throughout the world, it is the magi who are known as the "wise men."

The Paradox

This paradox sets the stage for the whole book of Matthew. Invariably, it is the least expected person who recognizes that Jesus is the messiah. Has Matthew sought out examples of all those against whom the Jews had some sort of ban? Prostitutes, sinners, publicans, lepers, lame, blind, and gentiles were all scorned by the religious Jews. After all, there are scriptural injunctions against their serving in the religious rituals and even against their entering into the temple. Undoubtedly, sicknesses must be punishment for sins and proof that the sick person is defiled in some way. Sinners and secular persons have condemned themselves by choosing not to follow the religious rituals. Even though many Gentiles are converting to Judaism, Gentiles are not really considered as worthy of the love of God. Why, there's even a special court for them in the temple and even God Himself has forbidden that they come any closer to the Holy Place. For sure, the Chosen is a very select group! Yet Matthew seems to have proof that it is precisely these ostracized persons who will enter the kingdom of God. How can the kingdom be open to them if even the temple is closed to them?

Jesus' public life is a ministry of preaching and healing which gathers unto Him a following of the sick, the demon-tortured, the lunatic, and the paralytic. (Matthew 4:24-25) The first person recorded by Matthew to have recognized Jesus as "Lord" and to call Him by the divine title is a leper. (Matthew 8:2) A centurion (an uncircumcised gentile, a foreign intruder, an enemy of Israel) expresses a faith which exceeds the faith of anyone in Israel. (Matthew 8:10) Even demons recognize Jesus as the son of God. (Matthew 8:29) As the blind call Him "son of David," He heals them. (Matthew 9:27-29) Jesus casts out devils, and the street people marvel and proclaim that these miracles have never been seen before in Israel. Looking on, the Pharisees say that Jesus is casting out these demons by the prince of devils. (Matthew 9:32-34) Again, Jesus casts out demons of blindness and dumbness as the street people look on in amazement. They proclaim that Jesus is the "son of David"; and, again, the Pharisees accuse Jesus of doing the miracles through the power of Beelzebub, the prince of demons. (Matthew 12:22-24) What a scene to behold! People are rejoicing not only at the miracle but also, at the fact they have finally found their long-awaited messiah! It is Christmas, New Years, and Fourth of July all rolled into one! But when the Pharisees arrive with their long faces and deathly accusation, a hearse is the only thing missing to complete the funeral scene.

Then, there is the little gentile lady from up near Tyre and Sidon. Her heart is broken because a devil had possessed her daughter, but she has one glimmer of hope -- Jesus can heal her daughter. But will He? In Him, she recognized the messiah of Israel and also believes that He is truly the messiah of the whole world. Refusing to take "no" for an answer, she worships Jesus even when He tries to turn her aside. Then acknowledging her faith, He delivers the young girl. (Matthew 15:21-28)

Let the Party Begin

As Jesus travels around Israel, the scenes shift but the plot is the same. The setting is the only difference as Jesus continues to heal the sick and handicapped. The common folk always respond with praise to God, proving that they see Jesus as a man from God, not from Beelzebub. The fireworks of the Fourth of July seems to follow Jesus around! (Matthew 20:29-34) As He and His entourage enter Jerusalem, the greatest celebration yet breaks out. The street people throw their coats before the donkey on which Jesus rides. They wave palms and sing praises to God and Jesus -- calling Him "son of David." As usual, the Pharisees appear with their funeral procession of accusations against Jesus. This time Jesus answers them with a word from the scripture, "Out of the mouth of babes and suckling thou hast perfected praise." Was He trying to say that even the scriptures had prophesied that the ones least expected would recognize the messiah? (Matthew 21:8-16)

Finally, it comes time for the Pharisees to have their own Fourth of July celebration -- a real funeral. They plot and scheme until their plans are complete. The scheming involves every member of the Jewish religious system who can be trusted not to betray the plan. The Sanhedrin, the Sadducees, the scribes, the elders of Israel, the chief priests, and even the high priest take part with the Pharisees in planning the execution of this prophet called "son of David." Taking money out of the temple treasury, they pay false witnesses and buy a member of Jesus' own following as a betrayer.

With the plans complete, each part begins to fall together like clockwork. Everything is a rush job and much of it has to be done at night. Everything must be finished quickly -- before the Passover and before the street people realize what is happening and have a chance to spoil the plot. It all comes off just as planned. Even though the false witnesses tell conflicting stories, the jury somehow produces a guilty verdict. The Roman governor, Pontius Pilate, almost spoiled their plans because he felt that Jesus was really innocent. That, too, seemed to be calculated into the plans. Since it was Passover, the Romans were prepared for riots and uprisings. At holidays, and especially on Passover, Jewish patriotism runs high. Passover is a festival of deliverance which reaches a climax at the point in the Pascal meal when the worshipers literally expect the messiah to appear. Having learned from experience, the Romans doubled their forces in Jerusalem on Passover week. They had also learned that with the Jews, it was more expedient to prevent a religious uprising rather than to squelch it once it began. The plotters knew that they had Pilate "over a barrel." If he tried to save the life of one man, he would risk a full-scale revolution! Pilate tried one last-ditch effort by appealing to the people to release Jesus, but the religious leaders quickly swayed the crowd until they suddenly became a blood-thirsty mob calling for Jesus' death. It was working! Everything was fitting together according to the plans of the Jewish leaders! Rejoicing, they slapped one another's backs and called each other "wise."

Now was their time to get back at this religious fanatic who had caused them so much trouble. He had allowed all the cripples, insane, uneducated, poor, and less-than-kosher Jews to call Him their king. Now they were going to prove what kind of king He really was. They stripped Him, robed Him in scarlet, and gave Him a reed as a scepter and thorns for a crown. Beating Him, spitting upon Him, and mocking Him, they called him "king of the Jews." They taunted Him to prophesy to them who it was that was hitting Him. They derided Him to deliver Himself by His kingly power. Crucifying Him they marked His cross with the accusation, "King of the Jews." Standing at the foot of His cross, they scoffed at the king of Israel nailed to a tree and the son of God dying as a criminal. Even the two criminals being crucified with Him took part in the hideous mockery. In spite of suffering agony beyond description, they mustered their strength and gasped for a breath to mock and jeer at this powerless king.

Just as the Pharisees had always turned the believers' celebrations into funerals, suddenly, their funeral-celebration lost all its festive spirit. This time,

God Himself crashed the party. The sun turned to darkness, the earth quaked, graves opened, rocks crashed, and the crucified king was dead. One of the Roman soldiers who had been in charge of the execution -- a rough, uncircumcised enemy of Israel -- suddenly realized what was happening and cried out, "Truly this is the Son of God." Again the great paradox: the first to recognize that the crucified Jesus was the Son of God was a man from outside Israel -- a man who was in no way a partaker in the covenant or promise of God. This pagan was the only one to recognize the promise when it was fulfilled and to recognize the covenant when the covenant blood was shed. In Bethlehem and at Golgotha, only Gentiles recognized the king of the Jews!

Jesus--Messiah for the Gentiles?

Surely, this new Christian religion will soon be a thing of the past in Israel. Certainly, it is the gentiles who are meant to be Christians. After all, they are always the wise ones and the Jewish leaders always wind up playing the part of the fool in Matthew's book. Notice especially the really hard blow near the end of Matthew where Judas returned his pay-off money to the priests. That one really makes them look like fools because they saw nothing wrong with taking blood money out of the treasury but find it sinful to put the same blood money back into the same treasury.

Certainly, Matthew must hate the Jews for having killed his Jesus. But there is one more chapter to go, and it's all about the resurrection. That is the biggest part of the controversy over this Jesus and His religion. Maybe there is a final clue to the whole controversy in that chapter. There it is -- this risen Christ told His disciples to go preach to the nations -- that means gentiles! Good, the Jews are off the hook, Christianity really is a Gentile religion! The book is closed -- but not for long. Somewhere in the story, Matthew has woven in enough facts to make even a Jewish reader curious as to whether Jesus really is the son of David and the son of Abraham. Since everyone wants to be wise and not a fool, the book must be re-read.

Maybe Matthew really doesn't hate the Pharisees and other religious Jews. Maybe he's just trying to get across a point. Perhaps this Jesus of his had something to say about the way the rabbis and leaders are interpreting their religion. After all, the book is packed full of quotations from the Hebrew scriptures and allusions to rabbinical interpretations of the scriptures. Maybe there really is something to the way Matthew interprets these passages. Maybe the Pharisees are wrong. No matter how serious they were, they may just be missing the point of the scriptures.

From the first, Matthew seems to imply that he has a totally different interpretation of what it means to be a Jew. He quotes John the Baptist in saying that the true sons of Abraham are not those who have Abraham for an ancestor, but rather those who show forth fruits worthy of repentance. John even went so far as to say that God could raise up sons of Abraham from the stones. (Matthew 3:7-10) That's a pretty radical statement but it does seem to ring of the prophet Micah who said that God wasn't pleased with sacrifices and religious ritual but looked for a man who would "do justly, love mercy and walk humble before God." (Micah 6:6-8) In fact, Jesus even quoted that verse to the Pharisees in one of their discussions. (Matthew 12:7) It even sounds like the words of the rabbi who told a gentile that he could recite the whole

Torah while standing on one foot. The gentile vowed to become a proselyte if the rabbi could fulfill his promise. The rabbi then stood on one foot and said, "Love thy neighbor as thyself and God will all thy might, strength, soul, and spirit." Maybe Matthew and Jesus are trying to say that if the Jews would return to this simple understanding of the Torah they could be wise and not fools. They could be true sons of Abraham in a spiritual sense.

After all, every time Jesus and the Pharisees clashed, the conflict seemed to be centered around some point where the Pharisees had let their ritual purity become more important than justice, mercy, and humility before God. Jesus didn't mind pointing out the Pharisees' shortcomings. He called them hypocrites every time He saw them breaking their own Torah. Maybe He was being cruel, but really it seems more likely that He was trying to correct rather than to punish them. He calls them hypocrites when they give alms because their intentions are on being seen giving rather than in helping the poor. (Matthew 6:2) He calls them hypocrites when they pray because they make a spectacle for onlookers rather than really communing with God. (Matthew 6:5) They are hypocrites in fasting (Matthew 7:5), in keeping Jewish rituals at the expense of honoring father and mother (Matthew 22:18), in predicting the weather but not being able to interpret the scripture (Matthew 16:3), and in asking questions about man's responsibility because really they are trying to trick Jesus rather than find a serious answer (Matthew 22:18). He pronounces woes and sorrows on these hypocritical scribes and Pharisees because they know the observances commanded by God and even repeat them but do not live by them. (Matthew 23:2-38) He proclaims that the final end of the hypocrites will be weeping and gnashing of teeth in torment. (Matthew 24:51) But in all of His accusations against the Jewish leaders, there seems to be a tone of love rather than hate. Jesus seems not to hate the men, but to hate only the cruel and hypocritical way they destroy the Torah. The true heart of Jesus is revealed when He laments that He wants to call them under His wings but they refuse. It is not Jesus that rejects the Jews; it is the Jews that reject Him!

Jesus seems to say that His followers should start where the scribes and Pharisees leave off. Jesus wants His followers to observe the teachings of the Pharisees, but He warns them against the attitude and actions of these Jews. (Matthew 23:3) He commands His followers to exceed the righteousness of the scribes and Pharisees in fulfilling the intent of the Torah rather than merely its letters. (Matthew 5:20) Jesus claims that He Himself is the fulfillment of the law and prophets. He claims not to be destroying the faith and promise of the Jewish scripture -- rather He claims to be fulfilling them in a deeper spiritual sense than the Jews have been able to understand. (Matthew 5:17) He commands His followers to live by all the Ten Commandments and to go one step further in the sacrificing of their own possessions to help the poor. (Matthew 16:22) He challenges them to live not by the letter of the law but to also understand that the intent of the law begins with the attitude of the heart. He tells us that God is as concerned about hatred as He is about murder. (Matthew 5:21-22) With adultery, divorce, swearing, revenge, and attitudes toward enemies, Jesus commands that His followers not stop at the letter of the Torah or rabbinical interpretation of the scripture but rather live by that principle. (Matthew 5:27-44) Then they can know that they are much more than sons of Abraham -- they will be sons of the Father in heaven! They will be much more than kosher -- they will be perfect! (Matthew 5:45-48) That's what all the Jewish ritual religion is all about -- but where did they miss it? Jesus says, "You do err, not knowing the scripture, nor the power of God." (Matthew 22:29) The scripture and the power of God -- maybe that's why Matthew spends so much time quoting the Hebrew prophets and describing Jesus' miracles!

The Scripture and the Power of God

In his short, little book, Matthew quotes Hebrew scriptures almost fifty times and has several other allusions to the Jewish scriptures and the Talmud. What seems to be the key to Matthew's understanding of the Jewish religion? Well, first of all, it seems that Matthew sees Jesus as the explicit fulfillment of the Hebrew prophecies. From almost insignificant points like what towns Jesus visited (Matthew 4:13-16 fulfilling Isaiah 9:1-2) to His ministry in the role of messiah (Matthew 12:14-21 fulfilling Isaiah 42:1-4), every action seems to have been prophesied. Some of the prophecies He could have deliberately set out to fulfill; but many, like the dice game for His garment at His crucifixion (Matthew 27:35 fulfilling Psalms 22:18), were completely beyond His control. Matthew believes that God is the one who made Jesus' life to perfectly coincide with the ancient prophecies. Maybe so, or maybe it is only a string of coincidences -- could Jesus have been just the victim of a lot of circumstances? He was born of a virgin (Matthew 1:23 fulfilling Isaiah 7:14), He had a star which announced His coming (Matthew 2:2 fulfilling Numbers 24:17), He was born in Bethlehem (Matthew 2:4-6 fulfilling Micah 5:2), He spent part of His childhood in Egypt (Matthew 2:14-15 fulfilling Hosea 11:1), His birth triggered the massacre of many children in the area of Ramah (Matthew 2:16-18 fulfilling Jeremiah 31:15), He grew up in Nazareth (Matthew 2:23 fulfilling Isaiah 11:1 -- this is a rabbinic play on the word "Branch" [pronounced Nezer] which connects the messianic promise with the city of Nazareth), His ministry was announced by John the Baptist who proclaimed the fulfillment of Isaiah's prophecy (Matthew 8:17 fulfilling Isaiah 53:4), He preached in the Galilee area (Matthew 4:13-16 fulfilling Isaiah 53:4), He healed the sick (Matthew 8:17 fulfilling Isaiah 53:4), the validity of His ministry was proven in the healing of the blind, the cripples, the lepers, and the deaf, and in the preaching of the gospel to the poor (Matthew 11:4-5 fulfilling Isaiah 42:1-4), the sign of His authority was His three-day stay in the grave (Matthew 12:38-40 fulfilling Jonah 1:7), He spoke in parables so that those who would understand could, and those who would not understand could not (Matthew 13:13-15 fulfilling Isaiah 6:9), His ministry was preceded by that of John the Baptist (Matthew 17:10-13 fulfilling Malachi 4:5), He entered Jerusalem riding a donkey (Matthew 21:1-5 fulfilling Zechariah 9:9), when He was killed, His disciples were scattered (Matthew 26:31 fulfilling Zechariah 13:7), He was crucified (Matthew 26:31 fulfilling Psalms 22 and Isaiah 52:13 and 53:12), He was captured as if He were a criminal (Matthew 26:55-56 fulfilling Lamentations 4:20), His blood money was used to buy a potter's field (Matthew 27:3-10 fulfilling Zechariah 11:12), and His executioners gambled for His clothes (Matthew 27:35 fulfilling Psalms 22:18).

That centurion at the cross must be right in his proclaiming, "Truly, this was the son of God." It is impossible for one man to have so perfectly fulfilled the prophecies of so many prophets unless he really is sent by God. Matthew is not bashful to say that Jesus is fulfilling the role of the servant of God. Those servant passages in Isaiah are undisputed as references to the messiah. He doesn't hesitate to equate Jesus with the king of Israel in Zechariah 9:9 or the tortured witness of Psalm 22. Matthew made a terribly bold claim for Jesus, but he seems to have evidence to back it up. Then, again, Jesus Himself is not too bashful in claiming His authority. He claims to be fulfilling all the law and the prophets. (Matthew 5:17) He claims that He is manifesting God's presence in a way that the prophets and righteous men of the past would have desired to have seen. (Matthew 13:17) He claims to be equal to David. (Matthew 12:1-4) He claims to be Lord of the Sabbath. (Matthew 12:8) He claims to be greater than Solomon. (Matthew 12:42) He refused to silence the crowd when they proclaimed Him to be the messiah by quoting the messianic acclamations from Psalms 118:25. (Matthew 21:8-16) He claims that His works proved His authority in such a powerful way that even the wicked cities of Tyre, Sidon, and even Sodom would have repented. (Matthew 11:20-24) To top it all, He tells the chief priest that He will come in the clouds on the right hand of power -- sort of a Jewish code word for messiahship. (Matthew 26:63)

Kingdom of Jesus--Kingdom of God
     If Jesus really is the messiah, why didn't He deliver Israel from Rome? Why didn't He set up His kingdom? Why did God allow the messiah to be killed? And when He came back to life -- if that's what really happened -- why didn't He set up His kingdom then? Well, maybe He is a different kind of messiah. After all, it's beginning to be clear that "wise ones" of Israel have

some pretty foolish ideas about the whole meaning of their religion. If they missed the point of man's responsibilities toward God and one another -- maybe, just maybe, they misunderstood the meaning of their coming messiah. Maybe the messiah is promised as some sort of spiritual deliverer rather than a political savior. If this is the case, then the story about His forty-day fast and temptation begins to take on a whole new meaning.

Right at the first of the book, Jesus has just stepped out into the public eye. John the Baptist baptized Him and God Himself spoke from heaven saying, "This is my beloved son, in whom I am well pleased." (Matthew 3:17) That sounds a lot like Psalms 2:7 -- an enthronement Psalm which is often associated with the messiah. Then Jesus goes out into the wilderness and fasts for forty days. Enter stage right, Satan who begins to tempt Jesus. First, he tries to get Jesus to make bread for Himself out of the rocks. Jesus refuses saying that He must depend on God, not on physical things. He quotes Deuteronomy 8:3 to make His point. Next, Satan tries to get Jesus to prove His dependence on God by jumping from the pinnacle of the temple. Jesus refused that temptation by pointing out the difference between trusting God and tempting Him. Deuteronomy 6:16 is His verse this time. Finally, Satan tries to tempt Jesus by offering Him all the earthly kingdoms. That offer really goes against the messianic promise in the enthronement Psalm -- it says there that God will give the messiah the kingdoms, not that He will have to win or earn them. (Psalms 2:8) More than that, it means that Jesus would be turning His trust from God to Satan and his bargain. Jesus again turns to the book of Deuteronomy (verse 6:13) for a response. Exit Satan stage left. It seems that the whole point of the visit from Satan is to try to get Jesus to manifest His messiahship in some physical way, but Jesus consistently refuses because He knows that His kingdom is a spiritual one based upon dependence on God. With the temptation over, Jesus goes out to the villages and begins to preach repentance in preparation for the coming kingdom (Matthew 4:17). That word "repent" really seems to push the kingdom into a spiritual realm rather than into an anti-Roman political machine!

It's also interesting how He always found an answer in Deuteronomy -- perhaps there's a connection with the fact that Deuteronomy also contains the verse which He called the greatest commandment, "Thou shalt love the Lord thy God with all thy heart, and with all thy soul, and with all thy mind. This is the first and great commandment. And the second, is like unto it. Thou shalt love thy neighbor as thyself. On these two commandments hang all the law and prophets." (Matthew 22:37:40) He seems to say that the zenith of Jewish religion is not a free Israeli state, but rather a nation of spiritually free people who trust God and prove it in worship of God and love toward neighbors. He gives a little rule for testing to see if this zenith has been reached, "Therefore all things whatsoever you would that men should do to you, do ye even so them: For this is the law and the prophets." (Matthew 7:12) The great Jewish rabbi, Hillel, had given a very similar rule but he called it the fulfillment of the Torah, the Law. Jesus, on the other hand, recognizes the obligation for man to live a perfectly holy life but states that it is God's promise that He will make man able to live that perfectly holy life. What a difference between Jesus and the rabbis! Maybe there really is something supernatural about Him! Maybe He is the son of David,

32

the son of Abraham!

There really is a difference in the way He talks about God. It is apparent in the way the people responded to His teaching. "The people were astonished at his doctrine: For he taught them as one having authority, and not as scribes." (Matthew 7:28-29) But what is this authority? It is apparent that He didn't have to have someone else to confirm His teaching. All the rabbis would make a statement and wait for another rabbi to confirm it with the word "amen," but Jesus seems to have some self-contained authority with which He confirms His own statements.

This Jesus, who can "amen" His own statements, seems not to be presenting facts and concepts about God and His kingdom. Rather, He seems to actually be manifesting God and the kingdom through His own ministry and person. That's where He gets His authority! He is not the messenger of the kingdom, He is the very presence of the kingdom! He even claimed that if He casts out devils by the Spirit of God that the kingdom of God has come. (Matthew 12:28) It was through contact with and trust in Jesus that people are changed so that they can be part of the spiritual kingdom which He manifested. All of Jesus' statements about the kingdom seem to culminate in the reality of lives changed through submission to God's rule of love. "Whosoever therefore shall humble himself as this little child, the same is the greatest in the kingdom of heaven." (Matthew 18:4) "Suffer little children, and forbid them not, to come unto me: for such is the kingdom of heaven." (Matthew 19:14) "It is impossible for a rich man, who would trust himself rather than God, to enter into the kingdom of heaven." (Matthew 19:23-26) "Amen I say unto you, that the publicans and the harlots go into the kingdom of God before you. For John came unto you in the way of righteousness, and ye believeth him not: But the publicans and the harlots believed him: And ye, when ye had seen it, repented not afterward that ye might believe him." (Matthew 21:31-32) "But woe unto you, scribes and Pharisees, hypocrites! For ye shut up the kingdom of heaven against men: For ye neither go in yourselves, neither suffer ye them that are entering to go in." (Matthew 23:13) "Repent for the kingdom of heaven is at hand." (Matthew 4:17) "Blessed are the poor in spirit: for theirs is the kingdom of heaven." (Matthew 5:3) "Many shall come from the east and west and shall sit down with Abraham, and Isaac, and Jacob, in the kingdom of heaven. But the children of the kingdom shall be cast out into outer darkness: There shall be weeping and gnashing of teeth." (Matthew 8:11-12)

That makes a lot of sense. Jesus has come to manifest a spiritual kingdom that has to do with getting one's heart right with God. His talk about repenting and having the attitude of a little innocent child is easy for the harlots, publicans, sinners, gentiles, and lepers to understand. They know they are wrong and need to repent. But the Pharisees and scribes have fooled themselves by doing so many religious things that they actually must feel that they are right. That's why the kingdom has to pass from their hands to the hands of the sick and sinful. The self-proclaimed wisdom and righteousness of the Jews keeps them out of the kingdom and the self-recognized sinfulness of the publicans wins them the kingdom. Here we have the paradox of wise men and fools again!

A Second Call?

But surely the kingdom isn't closed to the Jews

now, or else Matthew wouldn't have gone to the trouble to write such a Jewish-sounding story about Jesus. Maybe his gospel is a second call to the Jews who missed the first call. Maybe it's like the story Matthew records of the transfiguration. (Matthew 17:11-12) On that mountaintop, the disciples saw Jesus talking with Moses and Elijah -- symbols of the law and the prophets. At first the disciples could not understand the great vision because they had their eyes on all three. They wanted to build three tabernacles and stay on the mountain. But they looked again and saw only Jesus. It is as though God was trying to show them that Jesus is such a perfect fulfillment of the law and prophets that man needs to look only at Jesus for salvation. In fact, God spoke and commanded that they hear Jesus because He is the Son of God. Then with Jesus' touch, they are delivered from their fears and enabled to trust and follow Him. In writing this book, Matthew seems to be hoping that the same voice of God and touch of Jesus will help his readers see Jesus as the fulfillment of the law and prophets.

Certainly it is that same sort of experience that came to Peter at Caesarea Philippi when he recognized that Jesus was the Christ, the Son of the living God. (Matthew 16:13-16) Here, Jesus acknowledged that Peter had received this knowledge by revelation from God and spoke of that revelation and the heart change it produced as the rock upon which Jesus would build a church that hell itself could not withstand. (Matthew 16:17-18) What a proof of the presence of the kingdom of God!

Understanding of the word "rock" as standing for the revelation of Jesus as God's son gives meaning to Jesus' parable about the two men who build houses. (Matthew 7:24-27) One was wise and one was foolish.

The foolish built his house on sand and it fell. But the wise man established his life on the rock (revelation of Jesus as God's son) and it stood through "hell and high water." Oh, how wonderful to think that there is a solid footing upon which to build one's life. If only this Jesus were still alive. Oh, yes! He is still alive. In fact, Matthew makes it sound as if He is more alive after His death and resurrection than before! And He's here today with men so that we can choose to trust and follow Him! After His resurrection, Jesus came and spoke unto them, saying, "All power is given unto me in heaven and in earth. Go ye therefore, and teach all nations, baptizing them in the name of the Father, and of the Son, and of the Holy Ghost: teaching them to observe all things whatsoever I have commanded you: And, lo. I am with you always, even unto the end of the world. Amen." (Matthew 28:18-20)

Furthermore, He taught that He was to receive His position in the kingdom in a regenerated state -- not during his thirty-three-year sojourn on Planet Earth. "And Jesus said unto them, Verily I say unto you, That ye which have followed me, in the regeneration when the Son of man shall sit in the throne of his glory, ye also shall sit upon twelve thrones, judging the twelve tribes of Israel." (Matthew 19:28)

"Jesus saith unto him, Thou has said: nevertheless I say unto you, Hereafter shall ye see the Son of man sitting on the right hand of power, and coming in the clouds of heaven." (Matthew 26:64)

The Davidic Promise Fulfilled

This re-entry into human affairs will be the ultimate fulfillment of the promise to David that his seed would be given a permanent throne in Jerusalem.

As our Jewish host has found, the hero in the

Gospel of Matthew is always the one who could have been voted "least likely to succeed." This is what the New Testament as a whole teaches when it says that God has chosen the foolish things to confound the wise. (I Corinthians 1:27) The wisdom of God is revealed every time an unbeliever turns to seek Christ. The foolishness of man is manifested every time we reject His revelation. Paul confirms that not only Jews, but gentiles alike, are guilty of this gross foolishness. "Because that, when they knew God, they glorified Him not as God, neither were thankful; but became vain in their imaginations, and their foolish heart was darkened. Professing themselves to be wise, they became fools." (Romans 1:21-22)

Be wise today. Embrace Jesus as the Lord of your life. Turn from the foolishness of letting anything else stand in the place of God in your life. Once you have embraced wisdom, share this new life with others. "The fruit of the righteous is a tree of life; and he that winneth souls is wise." (Proverbs 11:30) "And they that be wise shall shine as the brightness of the firmament; and they that turn many to righteousness as the stars for ever and ever." (Daniel 12:3)

Yes, Virginia, There is a ...

During the Christmas season of 1897, a short note to the editor appeared in <u>The</u> <u>New</u> <u>York</u> <u>Sun</u>. Virginia O'Hanlon wrote:

> Dear Editor: I am eight years old. Some of my friends say there is no Santa Claus. Papa says, "If you see it in <u>The</u> <u>Sun</u>, it's so." Please tell me the truth: is there a Santa Claus?

The editor's response was masterful as he wove his words to describe the magic of Christmas and the spirit of the season. He confirmed, "Yes, Virginia, there is a Santa Claus." The missive and its reply soon became a classic and made a place in journalism history.

Today, more than a century later, there seems to be little question concerning jolly old Saint Nick. Every mall, every product catalogue, every commercial, every street corner, and every television holiday special shouts at the top of its voice, "Yes, Virginia, there is a Santa Claus." A modern remake of the all-time movie favorite <u>The</u> <u>Miracle</u> <u>on</u> <u>34th</u> <u>Street</u> seems to sum up our feelings that there is a Santa Claus and that he is what makes Christmas so magical.

Somehow I wonder if Miss O'Hanlon would be writing the same letter were she to address the editor today. A more in-touch question might be:

> Dear Editor: I am eight years old. The ACLU, my school system, all I see in the stores and on TV, and all I hear from my little and big friends tells me that there is no Jesus. Please tell me the truth: Is there a Jesus?

I question if there are any writers left who could so

artistically and deftly answer our little friend's query as the Sun editor could have. But I would like to point you to just one special Christmas story and let history itself speak to us about the question. Amid the horrors of World War I, there occurred a unique truce when, for a few hours, enemies behaved like brothers.

Christmas Eve, 1914, was quiet on France's western front, from the English Channel to the Swiss Alps. Trenches came within fifty miles of Paris. The war was only five months old, and approximately eight hundred thousand men had been wounded or killed. Every soldier wondered whether Christmas Day would bring another round of fighting and killing. But something happened: British soldiers raised "Merry Christmas" signs, and soon carols were heard from German and British trenches alike.

Christmas dawned with unarmed soldiers leaving their trenches, as officers of both sides tried unsuccessfully to stop their troops from meeting the enemy in the middle of no-man's land for songs and conversation. Exchanging small gifts -- mostly sweets and cigars -- they passed Christmas Day peacefully along miles of the front. At one spot, the British played soccer against the Germans, who won 3-2.

In some places, the spontaneous truce continued the next day, neither side willing to fire the first shot. Finally the war resumed when fresh troops arrived, and the high command of both armies ordered that any further such "informal understandings" with the enemy would be punished as treason.

Here we have proof positive of the message proclaimed across the hills of Bethlehem by that great host of heaven, "Glory to God in the highest and on earth peace, good will to men!" The Prince of Peace of Isaiah 9:6, the King of Peace mentioned in Hebrews

7:2, the One who is Himself our Peace described in Ephesians 2:14, and the very God of Peace from Philippians 4:9 has come to earth and is present with us in the baby born on Christmas Day.

Yes, Virginia, there is a Jesus! Yes, ten thousand times ten thousand times -- yes, yes, yes! Yes, there is a Jesus.

Where's Waldo?

They can almost drive you crazy -- those Where's Waldo? puzzles. A zillion people are crowded on a beach, in a mall, or on a city street. Somewhere in the multitude, one lone skinny little guy named Waldo is lost. Your mission is to find him. The needle in the proverbial haystack may not be much more challenging.

At Christmas time, as we force our way through the throngs of shoppers, it's sometimes easy to identify with poor little Waldo. We might ask ourselves, "Where's Waldo? Where am I? Who am I? Where do I fit into this big picture?"

As everyone of us who has been in church Christmas plays knows, the first Christmas Day involved a "cast of thousands." As we reflect on who all those various "actors" were, perhaps we can find Waldo; perhaps we can find ourselves.

As we scan the maze of characters on our Where's Waldo on the First Christmas? puzzle, the first figure that catches our attention is King Herod. Now, we all know what he was doing on the first Christmas morning -- he was plotting a way to get rid of the Christ child. After having been appointed King of Judea by his political friends in Rome, he found a very warm unwelcome in Jerusalem. In fact, he spent his entire reign looking over his shoulder for possible assassins. He dotted the countryside with palaces and fortresses because he never felt safe lying down to sleep without a thick rock wall and a band of guards between himself and his enemies -- his own subjects and countrymen. No ordinary house was protection for him; he demanded protection on every turn. This poor, insecure man even executed a number of his own

41

family members in an attempt to protect his throne from any possible contender. Certainly, you can imagine how his stomach must have churned when the wise men appeared at his court inquiring about the birth of a new king for the Jews. With his pasted-on smile, he replied that once they found this new regent, he wanted to come join them in worship and obeisance to Him. Behind that smiling mask was a villain's grin as he schemed the death of this new babe.

When we scan across this picture, we wish to move on quickly, thinking that, for certain, this evil King Herod is not Waldo. But wait, maybe he should be studied a little more closely. Perhaps he does relate to today's Christmas scene. Perhaps we will see some of ourselves in this monarch. Perhaps he is Waldo. Our whole nation is making a deliberate attempt to take Christ out of Christmas. The US Postal Service, along with other governmental and many major corporations have told their telephone and computer e-mail operators not to address their clients with a Christmas greeting. Instead, they are to offer them a "happy holiday" or "season's greetings." Courthouse lawns and school plays are not permitted to present the Bethlehem story. The administration at one state university told all the secretaries to remove any Christmas decorations which contained any religious nature from their desks. One school even prohibited the students from bringing Christmas candy canes to the classroom because the crooked sticks are said to represent the shepherd's staffs and, therefore, were religious symbols. Our Post Master General has recently ruled that he would continue, at least temporarily, printing a Christmas stamp with the picture of the Madonna and Child -- not because it is a religious stamp, but because it is a commemoration of the great art work of famous artists of the past. A town in West Virginia Town continues to erect its nativity scene -- but without a baby in manger. In our public schools Christmas stories, pictures, and plays about Jesus have been prohibited; but many schools present "cultural programs" about Kwazaa (an African religious holiday which coincides with Christmas), Diwali (a Hindu religious festival which also falls at the same time of the year), and Hanukah (a Jewish religious festival which also shares the season). Although these holidays are religious in nature, it seems that the ACLU and other enemies of religion in public life are not concerned. In San Jose, CA, the city council banned a manger scene from a public park but spent half a million dollars on a statue to Quetzalcoatl, the Aztec god of human sacrifice. Apparently, it is only Jesus who threatens them. Like King Herod, they wish to take Christ out of Christmas. One government agency told me that the students in the college where I served as dean could be certified to receive their tuition benefits during the Christmas break if we listed the time off as "winter break"; if the holiday remained on the calendar as "Christmas break," the students would not be paid during the vacation. The country of Uruguay has replaced Christmas and Holy Week with Family Day and Tourism Week. Birmingham, England, has renamed Christmas 'Winterval.' It is intended to be a catchy phrase for December and New Year's festivities so there is no slur on anyone or any religious faith. The City Council's decision enraged Christian leaders, who called it silly and an example of "political correctness to avoid sensitivities that people do not have."

The world today is full of Herods who want to turn Christmas into Xmas. Perhaps we have found Waldo -- perhaps we have found ourselves -- in King Herod.

43

But let's keep looking. Two other characters in this first Christmas drama were Simeon and Anna who appeared at Jesus' circumcision. These two players were spiritually in-tune senior citizens who had awaited the appearance of the messiah. Both had invested years of their lives in their spiritual quest. Now, just as they were to play out their final roles on Planet Earth, the fulfillment of their hopes, dreams, and prayers had finally come. What rejoicing there must have been as they held in their arms the Desire of the Ages, the Savior of the World! I pray that in these two saints of God that we find Waldo -- looking for the appearing of the Lord Jesus.

Unfortunately, it is likely that we come a bit closer to finding Waldo lurking nearby among some of the others congregated in the temple that day. If we remember the story of Herod, there was a group of religious leaders who were called to his assistance at the visit by the time of the wise men. When the question was asked as to where the new Jewish king was to be found, the king turned to the chief priests and scribes for an answer. Their immediate response was that He would be found in Bethlehem. Imagine: the messiah of the Jews, the savior of the world, the focal point of all history, the intersection of heaven and earth was waiting for them only a few miles away, and they knew that He was there -- within their reach! The subject of all their prophetic studies, the object of all their prayers, the focus of all their anticipations was within easy access. Finally, God had given them the opportunity to turn hopes into reality, prayers into substance, and dreams into fulfillment! Yet, not a one of these religious leaders left his comfortable home to wind his way through the Judean hillside to find this Jesus who had come to their tiny Bethlehem! More than likely, these same men were in the temple eight days later when the baby Jesus was laid in the arms of Simeon and Anna for His dedication to God. Not only did they refuse to go to Him in Bethlehem, but they also missed Him when He came to them in their very temple. Very likely, these same priests and scribes who were summoned to Herod's palace to respond to the wise men's query were also busy with their religious charges at the temple while Jesus was being proclaimed as the crown jewel of the heavenly kingdom. All their hopes, all their dreams, all their prayers, and all their prophetic studies had finally come to pass right under their noses -- and they missed it! Their religion had kept them from relationship with God. Their ritual had kept them from reality. Their sacrifices had kept them from salvation. Their scholarly theology had kept them from simple truth.

Where's Waldo? Do we see him here among the priests and scribes? I'm afraid that many of us may find ourselves numbered among the religious who somehow never let the faith (as in a set of doctrines) become our faith (as in the personal experience of our heart). In the early years of this century, a French aerialist came to Niagara Falls and mystified his audiences with his high-wire acrobatics performed high above the churning waters of the deadly Niagara Gorge. It is said that he captivated his observers with one particular stunt of pushing a wheelbarrow across the wire. When he returned, he asked if the crowd believed that he could do it again with a man in the wheelbarrow. When he pointed to one gentleman in the crowd, the guest affirmed that he believed that the feat could be done. At that point, Blondine invited the observer to get into the passenger's seat! Suddenly, the dividing line between mental accent (the faith) and real heart acceptance (his faith) became clearly drawn. It has been said that many people will miss heaven by only eighteen inches -- the distance between their heads and their hearts. These scribes and priests prove to us the eternal significance of those tiny eighteen inches. Where's Waldo? Where are you? Do you see yourself in these priests and scribes?

The innkeeper is the next figure that catches our eyes as we study the Christmas puzzle. The Bible actually never mentions this hotelier per se; although we do learn that there was no room for the Holy Family as they sought refuge in Bethlehem. In fact, new exegetical studies have suggested that the overcrowded facility was actually not a guest house at all, but the guest room of one of Joseph's relatives who lived in their traditional family home in Bethlehem. With all their family members coming back to their ancestral home for the tax registration, other cousins or uncles had already claimed the spare bedroom, leaving Joseph to find housing in the cellar where the supply room and cattle stable were located. If this is actually the case, we come to an even more villainous figure -- no longer is this some cold-blooded businessman who cared nothing for the way-faring stranger; rather, it is a heartless relative, Joseph's own flesh and blood, who thrust him out. Image denying a pregnant cousin, already in labor, a place to give birth simply because you got to the comfortable, warm guest room first! Well, this nasty innkeeper -- or in-law, as the case may be -- could be Waldo. Let's take a look. Have you ever had a sale's clerk at the mall treat you as if it were a nuisance to have you in his store? Have you ever seen a child -- or adult, for that matter -- become obsessed with his gifts? Have you ever had an unwelcome greeting from a family member at the holiday reunion?

Maybe we do find Waldo in the innkeeper -- the Scrooge of Christmas -- who is too selfish and self-centered to let the spirit of the season, the spirit of joy and giving, get inside of him. Where's Waldo? Where am I? Do I find myself in this greedy innkeeper? Hopefully not. But unfortunately, too often -- yes.

The wise men may be good candidates for our Waldo quest. These were venerated sages of the East who willingly gave themselves to their search for the Christ of Christmas. In their native lands of the Near East, they were men of position and reputation before their trek to Jerusalem and Bethlehem. However, it is likely that they gave up all this and returned to their homes as outcasts. The original word which we translate as "wise men" is "magi," from which we get our English word "magician." They relied on magic, dark powers, and demonic influence to give them power over the king and members of the royal court. In the royal courts of their homelands, these magi served as advisors and counselors to the regent. Their prognostications, based on the zodiac and the positions of the stars, told the ruler when to attack, when to retreat, how to invest, and how to negotiate. But suddenly they announced that they were off to "chase the pot of gold at the rainbow's end." Certainly, the king and his courtiers must have looked at them a bit askew when they asked for leave to follow their dream to Palestine.

In addition, they were pursuing a new relationship with God among the Jews -- the God who condemned everything these men treasured: their astrology, their sorcery, and their magic. These were men who were willing to give up everything they had, everything they were, everything they believed, everything they ever hoped to be, and everything they stood for in their quest for the Christ of Christmas. Perhaps they returned to their homelands to find that they no longer had jobs, friends, positions, or respect in the community. Not only did they give their gold, frankincense, and myrrh; they gave their all -- they gave themselves. Have we found Waldo? Oh, how I hope so! How my heart craves to be the man who truly puts Christ as the treasure of his life and forsakes all else to obtain Him. As the Apostle Paul phrased it:

> Yea doubtless, and I count all things but loss for the excellency of the knowledge of Christ Jesus my Lord: for whom I have suffered the loss of all things, and do count them but dung, that I may win Christ, and be found in Him, not having mine own righteousness, which is of the law, but that which is through the faith of Christ, the righteousness which is of God by faith: that I may know Him, and the power of His resurrection, and the fellowship of His sufferings, being made conformable unto His death; if by any means I might attain unto the resurrection of the dead. Not as though I had already attained, either were already perfect: but I follow after, if that I may apprehend that for which also I am apprehended of Christ Jesus. Brethren, I count not myself to have apprehended: but this one thing I do, forgetting those things which are behind, and reaching forth unto those things which are before, I press toward the mark for the prize of the high

calling of God in Christ Jesus.
(Philippines 3:8-14)

Of course, we have to take some time to study the Holy Family huddled around that manger crib as we continue our quest for this illusive Waldo. In Mary we see the flawless image of purity and righteousness. Her story is very familiar to us: a virgin girl of spotless reputation and sincere devotion to God who was visited by an angel with the message that she was to receive an overshadowing of the Holy Spirit and would become pregnant with the very Son of God. At first dismayed and astonished, she willingly submitted herself to this divine plan even though it meant ridicule and rejection from those who would not understand. For two millennia, she has been portrayed as the hero of the Christmas story -- and rightly so. However, there is just one little nagging question that continues to come to my mind concerning the Blessed Virgin. It has to do with the family's journey to Jerusalem twelve years later. As they observed the Feast of Passover and toured the magnificent City of David, there were so many things to see and do, so many people to meet, so many sights, sounds, and smells to absorb. In the midst of all the excitement and confusion, they lost their son Jesus. Thinking Him to be traveling with cousins, aunts and uncles, or relatives -- Mary paid no attention to the fact that Jesus was not with them. Gradually her nonchalance turned to curiosity as she began to question exactly where her son was. Finally, it turned to panic when she realized that He was nowhere among the party of her relatives, friends, and neighbors. It took her three horrifying days to find the lost boy. Certainly, she began by looking in all the haunts where adolescent boys are usually found: the ball fields, the fishing holes, and the street vendors selling sweets and treats. Finally, she turned to the temple and found Him among the priests and elders of the country.   Jesus' reply to His mother when she scolded Him for getting lost and causing her so much concern was, "Did you not know that I must be about my Father's business?" The boy was curious as to why the temple had not been the first place she would have looked for Him.   Had she forgotten the angel's message? Had she forgotten the visits of the wise men and the shepherds?   Had she forgotten?   Oh, the tragedy of forgetting, but we humans are so good at it. We so often receive great blessings from God but soon go back to living mundane lives, forgetting that God Himself has visited us. We forget that we are changed men and women. We forget to put God in first place. We simply forget! Have we found Waldo? Have we found ourselves?

Joseph must be the next figure to catch our attention. He is a unique personality in human history, but one about whom we know very little. Other than his family tree and the events related to the birth of Jesus, the sojourn in Egypt, and the Passover journey to Jerusalem, we know almost nothing about this key player.   Apparently he died sometime before Jesus entered His public ministry since he is never mentioned during those three years of the Savior's life. I suppose that it is only natural to seek to fill in some of the missing spaces in the story of such a significant figure. One detail that concerns me would be how this man, as the breadwinner of his family, must have felt on that first Christmas morning. He was a young man who was just starting his family. Perhaps he had scrimped and scraped and saved every penny that he could in order just to afford to take Mary as his wife. Likely, he had not planned to have children right away. Recent statistics show that it costs $100,000 to raise a child through high school, not to mention an average of another $100,000 for college expenses. This unfortunate man was still reeling from the unexpected blow of the financial responsibility of his instant family when he was suddenly hit from the other side by the decree that a new tax was to be levied. Not only must he pay the tax, but he also had the added expenses of the journey to Bethlehem. In addition, we must remember that he would have to be away from his livelihood for an undetermined period of time to travel to his ancestral home for the tax registration and then wait for his wife and baby to recuperate and gain strength for the trip home. At that time, he didn't even know about the added detour into Egypt! Poor Joseph must have had much of the joy of that first Christmas eaten away with his concern for the expenses he was facing. Does that sound familiar? Have we found Waldo? Do you see yourself on Christmas morning with more charge slips that you know how to handle?

Jesus told a couple parables which might help us locate some of the first Christmas characters. In one of these parables, we learn about a pearl merchant who had spent his life seeking for the most perfect pearl on the market. When he finally found the "Hope Diamond" of the pearl trade, he willingly sold everything he owned to buy that treasured specimen. In this story, I see the wise men -- seekers of spiritual truth who willingly gave up all they had and ever hoped to obtain in order to embrace the Truth. In a parallel story, Jesus told us about a hired hand who was plowing in the field of some corporate farmer. This hourly plowhand was not out looking or seeking for a fortune but suddenly came upon a windfall in the form of a buried treasure. Suddenly, the work-a-day fellow became an aggressive investor. He rushed home and held the biggest yard sale that his community had ever seen. Then a "for sale" sign appeared on the front lawn. Soon, the plowhand appeared at the front door of the land owner with a bankroll in his hand and an offer on his lips. I'm certain that the farmer could not imagine what had happened to turn the minimum-wage plowhand into a land baron, but he willingly cut the deal with his former employee. In this story, I see the shepherds -- men who were just doing their daily chores trying to earn a day's dollar, when something startling and totally unexpected surprised them. When the angel told them of the messiah's coming, they left their sheep and their careers as they rushed to find Him. Having found Him, they went everywhere telling everybody all that they had experienced. The New King James Version says that they made it "widely known."

One last place I want to look for Waldo is on Shepherd's Hill just outside the town of Bethlehem. Here we find several young men who are willing to give themselves for the Christ child. It is here that I hope we find Waldo. I pray that it is among these lowly shepherds that I find myself. May the Christ of Christmas so affect me that I am ready and willing to leave behind the mundane and follow the Great Commission, heeding the command of that favorite Christmas tune, "Go tell it on the mountain that Jesus Christ is born!"

Visions of Sugarplums

Next to the Bible, one of my favorite pieces of literature is Clement C. Moore's A Visit of St. Nicholas written in 1822. One line of that little poem really grabbed me. It was the line which conjures up such a secure, serene picture of children with the blanket pulled tightly up to their faces as they sleep in innocent bliss. It's a scene into which each of us would wish to find our way. We all long to be nestled all snug in our beds while visions of sugarplums dance in our heads.

Unfortunately, that is exactly what has happened to far too great a percentage of the church today. We've crawled into the warm covers of the church and let the devil lull us to sleep with visions of sugarplums. All the while, the Holy Spirit's alarm clock is ringing out the message that now is not the time to sleep. "And that, knowing the time, that now it is high time to awake out of sleep: for now is our salvation nearer than when we believed. The night is far spent, the day is at hand: let us therefore cast off the works of darkness, and let us put on the armour of light." (Romans 13:11-12) "Wherefore he saith, Awake thou that sleepest, and arise from the dead, and Christ shall give thee light." (Ephesians 5:14)

Our minds have become so enthralled with visions of sugarplums and our blessings of prosperity that the real visions God wants to give us are crowded out. But what is a true vision from God? It bears six characteristics which are easily remembered in that they are represented in the letters of the word VISION.

V is for "vital." "Where there is no vision, the people perish: but he that keepeth the law, happy is he." (Proverbs 29:18) Every vision from God brings life to the people of God and lost humanity. Visions stir the body of Christ to move from lethargy and come alive. They stir the church to evangelism and soul winning. With visions of sugarplums dancing in our heads, we nestle all snug in our beds while the world around us rushes headlong into a Christless eternity.

I stands for "insight." "And the child Samuel ministered unto the LORD before Eli. And the word of the LORD was precious in those days; there was no open vision." (I Samuel 3:1) In the day of Eli, divine vision was not common; and, because of that, the nation of Israel was eventually branded as Ichabad, "the glory of God is gone." When there is no vision or insight into who God is and what He is doing, His glory cannot abide. When we really get an insight into the nature of God as Jehovah Rapha, we'll not allow disease to remain; as Jehovah Jireh, we'll not allow lack to remain; as Jehovah Shalom, we'll not allow conflict and contention to remain; as Jehovah Shama, we'll not allow fear, worry, and depression to remain; and as Jehovah Tsidqenu, we'll not allow sin to remain. Yet with visions of sugarplums, we have no power to drive away any of these bondages. The only thing that will go away is the glorious liberty of Christ.

S represents "showing." "And the LORD answered me, and said, Write the vision, and make it plain upon tables, that he may run that readeth it." (Habakkuk 2:2) A true vision from God gives direction. It must be shared. Any word from God is too awesome to keep to oneself. Jeremiah decided not to share his vision from God but found that it was like a fire burning him up from the inside out unless he let it out to the people. A sugarplum vision might dance in your head, but a vision from God will find its way to your lips.

"Intimacy" is represented by the letter I. "And I Daniel fainted, and was sick certain days; afterward I rose up, and did the king's business; and I was astonished at the vision, but none understood it." (Daniel 8:27) For Daniel, the vision was not a casual, nonchalant event. It affected every part of his being -- body, soul, and spirit. A true vision from God will have intimate effect upon you.   When you really catch a glimpse of hell or heaven or Jesus on the cross or God on the throne, your life will be shaken to its very core. You'll never be the same again.   The dance of sugarplums in your head cannot change you like that.

O denotes "our." "And it shall come to pass in the last days, saith God, I will pour out of my Spirit upon all flesh: and your sons and your daughters shall prophesy, and your young men shall see visions, and your old men shall dream dreams." (Acts 2:17) We live in the last days, and visions are for us. I've already mentioned that in the days of Eli visions were uncommon. But today, it is our privilege to live at the time when all young men and women have the opportunity to receive visions. If we don't receive, it's not God's fault -- it's ours.

N means "needs." "Whereupon, O king Agrippa, I was not disobedient unto the heavenly vision." (Acts 26:19) Paul's vision demanded action. Your vision and my vision will also demand action. Visions draw us into the hurts, fears, disappointments, problems, sorrows, sicknesses, sins, and needs of the world around us. A man or woman with a vision is the only one who can bring people out of their needs. Once you've seen a vision, you will never again be blind to human suffering. To be inactive or neutral is to be nestled snug in our cozy beds, but visions thrust us into the world of human need.

Let's determine that sugarplums will give way to true vision of the meaning of Christmas.

Something Old,
Something New,
Something Borrowed,
Something Blue

December is a popular month for weddings. I guess it is because the grooms are wanting the advantage of the whole year's tax deduction for only a few days of support. As I think of Christmas, I see that, in at least one way, the holiday has taken on the nature of a December wedding. It bears the symbolism of the traditional bridal attire which requires that each young maiden who graces the aisle wear something old, something new, something borrowed, and something blue.

If anything, Christmas is the season of things old. It is the time of year that we love to reminisce of all our memories of Christmases past. We remember those childhood journeys "over the river and through the woods to Grandmother's house," decorating the tree, baking Christmas cookies, the house filled with the aromas of all the delicious holiday foods, sneaking a peek under the tree and secretly shaking the packages trying to guess what is inside, staying up late listing for the pawing of reindeer hooves on the roof, waking early to see if Santa had come, and the singing of Christmas carols. These Christmas traditions are vitally important to us because they are the cement that hold families and friends together from one holiday to the next. In each generation, we must relive the traditions of the past and actively create new memories for the present generation to carry into the future.

Christmas is also about things new because Christmas is all about changes. As each holiday season comes, we realize that we as individuals are constantly changing and the season takes on a new aspect with each passing year. We go from the stage of eagerly looking for Santa Claus, to questioning if Santa Claus exists, to becoming Santa Claus. We mature from being the wide-eyed children on Christmas morning to becoming the starry-eyed parents. We advance from being the receivers to becoming the givers. As Christmases pass, we somehow shift the emphasis of the season from gifts to family and -- hopefully -- to Jesus. In II Corinthians 3:18, the Apostle Paul tells us that we are being "changed into the same image (of Christ) from glory to glory, even as by the Spirit of the Lord." The Holy Spirit manifests Himself as what we know of as the Christmas spirit to bring us to a place of change which is evident with each Christmas that we count.

Although we usually think of New Years as the holiday which epitomizes change, we should stop and remember that the first Christmas was all about change. King Herod wanted to refuse the change, so he tried to kill the baby which was to initiate it. On the other hand, the shepherds welcomed change and rushed to the stable to welcome the very baby which the king was trying to exterminate. In fact, it seems to me that there is a divine order in the two holidays being piggybacked; it is only because of the baby born on Christmas that can we expect ability to be new in a new year.

Christmas is also things borrowed. The pages of the New Testament open with the story of some very unusual foreigners coming to Israel to honor the newborn king. These were men whom the scriptures identify as magi, a title from which we get our modern word "magician." They were men of the dark arts, men who employed trickery, illusion, and possibly even demonic power. Yet, they have become a permanent part of our holiday celebration. In fact, our entire repertoire of Christmas symbols is a hodgepodge of items collected from very foreign cultures melted into one gala collage. The Christmas tree was invented by Martin Luther when he decided to entertain his children by bringing a tree inside and decorating it with candles to duplicate the beauty of the moonlight dancing on the icicles on the trees in their backyard. Cultures all over the world have borrowed this German innovation until we can now find palm trees which have never even heard of icicles adorned with twinkling Christmas lights. Holly and mistletoe came to us from the Norsemen, but the idea has spread around the world until today I get Christmas cards from places like India and Nepal with pictures of these evergreens and I wonder if the people who sent the cards have ever even seen the real thing. I've spent a few Christmases in some tropical climates and almost laughed aloud to hear them singing about white Christmases when the only white we could see was the sand on the beach or about people being dressed up like Eskimos when everyone was wearing a bathing suit or about the weather being frightful while we were enjoying perfect a eighty degrees with a cool ocean breeze. Christmas is filled with things which we have borrowed from every culture around the world because Jesus belongs to the whole world.

This is the message that the angels heralded on that first Christmas: good will to all men -- not just to the Jews, but to everyone. Christmas is the time when we must break out of our own little worlds and go beyond the comfort zone to touch a world which are foreign and unfamiliar to us -- perhaps through serving a meal at the local rescue mission, caroling at a nursing home, taking gifts to the children of the inmates at your local jail, packing a shoebox of toys and school supplies for a child in a third-world orphanage, or bringing a box of warm clothes to the residents at a nearby homeless center.

"Christmas Shoes," a Christmas song which became popular several years ago, tells the story of a little boy who wants to buy a pair of shoes for his mother who is expected to die that night. When I first heard this song, I thought, "Why is such a sad song becoming so popular on this most joyous of holidays?" Then I realized that from its very origin Christmas has been characterized by sadness. As mothers throughout the Bethel area wailed at the loss of their babies and toddlers, the prophet Simeon dedicated the baby Jesus in the temple with a warning to the mother that her very soul would be pierced with sorrow because of the infant she held in her arms. It isn't only Elvis Presley who sometimes has a blue Christmas. Henry Wadsworth Longfellow wrote the class Christmas carol, "I Heard the Bells on Christmas Day," about the death of his son who was killed in the Civil War. For all of us, there is a sad note to Christmas. Every Christmas gathering reminds us of those who are missing from the holiday celebration. Several Christmases ago as we were wildly ripping the wrappings of our Christmas gifts, the phone rang with the news that my uncle had just suddenly collapsed and died. That interruption in our festivities certainly gave us a new perspective as we opened the rest of our presents. It made us want to add a new song to the list of carols we love to sing: "Will the circle be unbroken in the sky, Lord, in the sky?"

As we remember the missing members of our families, we can be comforted with the scriptural promises of Revelation 21:4, "God shall wipe away all tears from their eyes; and there shall be no more death, neither sorrow, nor crying, neither shall there be any more pain: for the former things are passed away," I Thessalonians 4:13, "But I would not have you to be ignorant, brethren, concerning them which are asleep, that ye sorrow not, even as others which have no hope," and Ephesians 2:12, "Ye were without Christ, being aliens from the commonwealth of Israel, and strangers from the covenants of promise, having no hope, and without God in the world." Unlike those who have no hope, we are assured that the Lord Himself is waiting to wipe away our tears because we do have God with us in this world. In fact, that is the very message of Christmas: Emmanuel, God with us, has come!! It's okay for us to feel a little blue in our Christmases because blue also symbolizes heaven in the Bible. The story of Christmas is that heaven sent its best gift to earth so that we can continue to enjoy the best gifts we have known on earth when we get to heaven.

As we enjoy this Christmas season, let's become the bride who is properly adored for her husband (Revelation 21:2) by paying attention to something old through treasuring the traditions which bind together our families, adorning ourselves with something new through enriching the holidays with new and fuller meaning and significance, embracing something borrowed by reaching a little beyond our own common experience to encompass someone else's world, and by bracing ourselves for the blueness of Christmas by making a renewed dedication to winning our unsaved loved ones to Christ during this coming year so that they will be part of that unbroken circle in the sky.

MARY, MOTHER OF GOD

The central figure for most of the Christmas story is the virgin Mary. Approximately one billion people around the world greet her daily with the familiar, "Hail Mary, full of grace, blessed art thou among women!" The object of my Christmas contemplation on Mary is to discover what lessons we can learn from her life.

My first consideration is that she had a divine connection.

> Now the birth of Jesus Christ was on this wise: When as his mother Mary was espoused to Joseph, before they came together, she was found with child of the Holy Ghost. (Matthew 1:18)

In Mary's case, she had the unique position of being called upon to be the mother of our Lord Jesus. However, just as she was privileged to bear Jesus in her womb, we are also privileged to bear Him in our hearts. Just as her pregnancy showed a little more each day throughout the gestation period until she was, as the gospels record, "great with child," we too should show a bit more each day that Christ is developing inside us. The Apostle Peter said that we should become partakers of the actual divine nature. Paul declared that we should demonstrate the workmanship of God in our lives so that our lives bring praise to the glory of God that is working through us. Jesus Himself said that our good works should be so evident before men that they will glorify the Father for what they see in our lives. We must have a divine connection which becomes apparently obvious as it did in Mary's life.

The second point of my consideration is that Mary very much maintained her human status.

> Is not this the carpenter's son? is not

his mother called Mary? and his
brethren, James, and Joses, and
Simon, and Judas? (Matthew 13:55)
And they said, Is not this Jesus, the
son of Joseph, whose father and
mother we know? how is it then that he
saith, I came down from heaven?
(John 6:42)

Even though the people had seen very unusual
things in the life of Jesus, they tried hard to convince
themselves that He was nothing special. In their quest
for proof that this hometown boy was nothing out of the
ordinary, they documented their evidence with the
statement that He was just Mary's son. Even though
she was the divinely appointed mother of the Savior,
Mary was still very much in touch with the reality of the
everyday world she lived in. Unfortunately, we
Christians today often tend to act like we are from a
different planet. Although we are taught that our true
citizenship is in heaven and that we are to exert the
rights and privileges of that citizenship while we live in
this world, we must not become alienated from the
present world and the people around whom we live.
We must live lives which are ordinary enough that
others can relate to us, yet extraordinary enough to
show that we do have something which those around
us are lacking.

My third thought would concern Mary's divine
recognition.

And the angel said unto her, Fear not,
Mary: for thou hast found favour with
God. (Luke 1:30)

When we read the story of the angelic appearance to
Mary, we can quickly see that God saw more in her
than Mary saw in herself. Even though she recoiled in

fear at the celestial visitation and, feeling her inadequacy, questioned the validity of his message, the heavenly guest insisted that God had seen something inside her which she had overlooked or failed to consider. So it is with us; we must remember that He looks at us through the eyes of love which thinks no evil and rejoices over truth rather than iniquity. He sees the best in us because He loves us so much. We must learn to see ourselves from God's perspective -- not making excuses for our faults or thinking that we have a license to continue in imperfection -- but focusing on God's unconditional love and acceptance.

In light of the last thought, we come to the next point in our consideration of the blessed mother's life: her sanctification.

> Then said Mary unto the angel, How
> shall this be, seeing I know not a man?
> (Luke 1:34)

Mary had carefully guarded her virginity and knew that she maintained moral purity. The same is true for our lives; even though we must learn to see ourselves thought the forgiving eyes of Christ, we must also do all that is within our ability to establish, maintain, and protect integrity in our moral and spiritual lives.

Probably the most important factor in Mary's life was submission.

> And Mary said, Behold the handmaid
> of the Lord; be it unto me according to
> thy word. And the angel departed from
> her. (Luke 1:38)

Certainly, she had "better" things to do with her life than to submit to an unwanted and untimely pregnancy. It almost cost her her marriage, and it certainly cost her her reputation in the community; but because she knew that it was the will of God, she humbly submitted to His plan.

In our lives, we often have our own agendas which must be altered. We often have certain things which seem valuable to us, but they must be surrendered in exchange for the invaluable will of God. Submission under the mighty hand of God is the master key to success.

Worship is another characteristic which we see demonstrated in the life of the holy virgin.

> And Mary said, My soul doth magnify
> the Lord, And my spirit hath rejoiced in
> God my Saviour. (Luke 1:46-47)

In her soul, her mental capacity, she magnified the Lord -- deliberately trained herself to see Him as bigger and more powerful than her natural inclination would be; but in her spirit, the part of her that has direct communication with God, she worshipped Him. Worship is higher than thanksgiving and more noble than praise; it is an expression of intimacy and ultimate abandon. We too must come to that place where our inmost parts continually express adoration to and passion for God.

Another trait we can readily discern in Mary was her meditative or reflective quality.

> But Mary kept all these things, and
> pondered them in her heart. (Luke
> 2:19)

We are commanded to meditate on the Word of God at all times; this incubation process is an important, yet often overlooked, part of spiritual development. Just as the embryo in the egg cannot mature into a chick outside the incubator, the truths of the Word of God will not become reality in our lives unless we give them time to gestate inside our spirit through reverent meditation and reflective contemplation.

Mary also demonstrated divine strength to deal with human conflict.

> And Simeon blessed them, and said unto Mary his mother, Behold, this child is set for the fall and rising again of many in Israel; and for a sign which shall be spoken against; (Yea, a sword shall pierce through thy own soul also,) that the thoughts of many hearts may be revealed. (Luke 2:34-35)

If Paul who had endured shipwrecks, beatings, stonings, imprisonments, ambushes, and countless other hardships could declare that he could do all things through Jesus Christ who strengthened him, we can also be assured that there is a source of strength outside ourselves to enable us to face the perplexities of life. Even though a sword may pierce our very souls, we can rely upon the same strength which sustained Paul and Mary.

Perseverance is the quality which is demonstrated when that divine strength meets the skirmishes of life.

> Now there stood by the cross of Jesus his mother, and his mother's sister, Mary the wife of Cleophas, and Mary Magdalene. (John 19:25)

When the multitudes who had been healed and fed, the disciples who had been nurtured, and even the inner circle (except for John) who had been mentored abandoned Jesus, only Mary and a handful of women remained with Him at the cross. Our only guarantee for success is faith with the tenacity of a bulldog which never gives up.

Mary's vision for the future is demonstrated in her presence on the Day of Pentecost.

These all continued with one accord in
prayer and supplication, with the
women, and Mary the mother of Jesus,
and with his brethren. (Acts 1:14)

Our last record concerning Mary's life is that she
was among those gathered in the Upper Room
awaiting the outpouring of the Holy Spirit. She had
been a vital part of one era of history, the physical
earthly sojourn of Jesus; but it had now ended. Yet,
she pro-actively moved into the next dimension, the
church age signified by the coming of the Holy Spirit.
Too often, we humans are not willing to accept change
and move forward into the future. But if we are to
follow Christ, we must have vision enough to see where
He is leading and courageously march forth.

Mary's life also highlighted a careful balance of
divine direction and human wisdom.

And when they were departed, behold,
the angel of the Lord appeareth to
Joseph in a dream, saying, Arise, and
take the young child and his mother,
and flee into Egypt, and be thou there
until I bring thee word: for Herod will
seek the young child to destroy him.
(Matthew 2:13)

Following both the divine messenger and her own
common sense, Mary escaped the murderous hand of
the king. We must also learn to use our heads and our
hearts when making decisions.

The holy mother had a tenacity to reclaim what
was lost.

Saying, Arise, and take the young child
and his mother, and go into the land of
Israel: for they are dead which sought
the young child's life. (Matthew 2:20)

As soon as she knew that it was safe to return to her homeland, Mary set out to reclaim her home, property, possessions, and heritage. No matter how easy it might have been to settle permanently in Egypt, Mary was not about to give up what rightfully belonged to her. We must also learn to lay hold to everything which is ours through the promises of God and take back any and everything which has been denied us.

The spiritual relationship between Jesus and His mother was more significant than their physical relationship.

> While he yet talked to the people, behold, his mother and his brethren stood without, desiring to speak with him. Then one said unto him, Behold, thy mother and thy brethren stand without, desiring to speak with thee. But he answered and said unto him that told him, Who is my mother? and who are my brethren? And he stretched forth his hand toward his disciples, and said, Behold my mother and my brethren! (Matthew 12:46-49)

Although this passage may seem to indicate disrespect on the part of Jesus for His mother, we know that He would not have violated the Ten Commandments by dishonoring His mother; therefore we must look a bit deeper to get its full meaning. In fact, the passage never says that Jesus refused His mother; He simply said that the deepest relationship she could have with Him would be to do the will of the heavenly Father -- something that Mary is portrayed as doing continually, though the brothers are pictured in a totally different light because they tried to lure Jesus into a trap early in His ministry. This passage speaks to us concerning our need to seek after spiritual relationships which, like the friend who sticks closer than a brother, are secure and enduring.

In line with the Abrahamic covenant, Mary was blessed so that she could be a blessing to others.

> And whence is this to me, that the
> mother of my Lord should come to me?
> (Luke 1:43)

As soon as she realized that she was pregnant, Mary went to spend time with her cousin Elizabeth who was also pregnant with John the Baptist. In that she returned to Nazareth during the last months of her pregnancy, it is apparent that her trip was not to hide herself from the local community. If it were, she would have waited until she was unable to hide the pregnancy before leaving for her cousin's house. Instead, she did exactly the opposite and returned home just when it would be impossible for her to disguise her condition. Obviously, Mary went to Elizabeth's home to assist the woman who found herself with child in her elderly years. Not only was she a physical helper, her presence proved to be a spiritual refreshment and encouragement to the saintly woman. As Christians, we must follow the example of Jesus who taught us to serve rather than be served. Whatever resources we have received -- finances, talent, etc. -- were given to us so that we can invest them in others. Paul aptly summed up our position when he said that he was willing both to spend and be spent for the sake of the brethren.

As spiritual as she might have been, Mary's human side had difficulty comprehending the divine.

> And Joseph and his mother marvelled
> at those things which were spoken of
> him. (Luke 2:33)

We can gain a little consolation at this point because we too have those moments when it is just too hard to really grasp hold of the spiritual dimension that the Lord would bring us into. It is encouraging to see that even the greatest of the biblical heroes had similar moments of hesitation. Our solace is in the fact that the Lord remembers our frame and takes into account the fact that we are made of mere dust.

On at least one occasion, Mary found it easy to level off into her physical nature and neglect the spiritual dimension.

> And when they had fulfilled the days, as they returned, the child Jesus tarried behind in Jerusalem; and Joseph and his mother knew not of it. But they, supposing him to have been in the company, went a day's journey; and they sought him among their kinsfolk and acquaintance. And when they found him not, they turned back again to Jerusalem, seeking him. And it came to pass, that after three days they found him in the temple, sitting in the midst of the doctors, both hearing them, and asking them questions. And all that heard him were astonished at his understanding and answers. And when they saw him, they were amazed: and his mother said unto him, Son, why hast thou thus dealt with us? behold, thy father and I have sought thee sorrowing. And he said unto them, How is it that ye sought me? wist ye not that I must be about my Father's business? And they understood not

the saying which he spake unto them. And he went down with them, and came to Nazareth, and was subject unto them: but his mother kept all these sayings in her heart. (Luke 2:43-51)

When she acted like a normal mother and looked in all the usual places for her missing son -- possibly the ball park, the street vender stands, the markets and shops -- rather than the temple, she proved that she was human and that she saw Jesus as simply human. Just as she had to be shocked into the supernatural dimension, we often need to be prodded to get beyond our human limitations and begin to operate with a heavenly mentality.

Mary demonstrated her faith when she directed the embarrassed wedding hosts to Jesus.

And the third day there was a marriage in Cana of Galilee; and the mother of Jesus was there: And both Jesus was called, and his disciples, to the marriage. And when they wanted wine, the mother of Jesus saith unto him, They have no wine. Jesus saith unto her, Woman, what have I to do with thee? mine hour is not yet come. His mother saith unto the servants, Whatsoever he saith unto you, do it. (John 2:1-5)

Without ever having seen Him perform a miracle, Mary somehow knew that Jesus could supernaturally intervene to solve the problem at the reception. True faith is being able to believe without having previous proof. Jesus told Thomas after he had seen the Master's nail-scared hands that those who could believe without having seen in advance were the truly blessed ones.

Even though she was His mother, Mary knew that she had to be a follower of Jesus, not His leader.

> After this he went down to Capernaum,
> he, and his mother, and his brethren,
> and his disciples: and they continued
> there not many days. (John 2:12)

In listening to the prayers we often pray and observing the way we live our lives, it would be easy to believe that we think that we are in the "driver's seat" rather than the "passenger's seat." We make our plans and ask Him to bless them rather than asking Him to show us His plans. We chart our course and ask Him to be with us rather than allowing Him to guide us. Mary, on the other hand, chose to walk <u>with</u> Him as He picked the path.

In His dying moments, Jesus pointed out Mary's interdependence with others in the family of God.

> When Jesus therefore saw his mother,
> and the disciple standing by, whom he
> loved, he saith unto his mother,
> Woman, behold thy son! Then saith he
> to the disciple, Behold thy mother! And
> from that hour that disciple took her
> unto his own home. (John 19:26-27)

Mary needed John, and he needed her. As members of the Body of Christ, we are all dependent upon each other. Just as any individual part of our physical anatomies cannot exist independently of the rest of the body, so we as members of the spiritual Body of Christ must give to and receive from all the other parts.

The Madonna and Child is unquestionably the best loved portrayal of the virgin Mary because it so graphically pictures the most recognized characteristics in the virgin mother: compassion, love, and tenderness.

> And she brought forth her firstborn son,
> and wrapped him in swaddling clothes,
> and laid him in a manger; because
> there was no room for them in the inn.
> (Luke 2:7)

At first mention of her name, our minds always picture the mother with the swaddling-clad baby in her arms. Before we force ourselves to see her desperately seeking her lost son in the winding streets of Jerusalem, before we envision her begging for admission to the house where Jesus was ministering, before we imagine her sobbing at the foot of Golgotha, before we glimpse her speaking in an unknown tongue in the Upper Room -- we must always pass through the Bethlehem stable. How fitting it is that Jesus said that this one quality is also the one by which we as Christians are to be identified: love.

When the angel Gabriel visited Mary, he addressed her as "highly favoured" (Luke 1:28) using the Greek word <u>charitoo</u> which appears only one other time in the New Testament. Paul uses this same word in Ephesians 1:6 when he says that we are accepted in the beloved. In other words, God's viewpoint on you and me is that He sees us in the same light as He saw the virgin Mary on the day He picked her to bear His son. We are accepted and favored so that we, too, can carry the very son of God in our lives.

The Needle in the Haystack

Let's to take a few minutes to reflect on the mystery of the incarnation of Jesus -- the hard-to-comprehend truth that Jesus was one hundred percent God yet became one hundred percent man.

> In the beginning was the Word, and the Word was with God, and the Word was God. The same was in the beginning with God. All things were made by him; and without him was not any thing made that was made. In him was life; and the life was the light of men. And the light shineth in darkness; and the darkness comprehended it not. There was a man sent from God, whose name was John. The same came for a witness, to bear witness of the Light, that all men through him might believe. He was not that Light, but was sent to bear witness of that Light. That was the true Light, which lighteth every man that cometh into the world. He was in the world, and the world was made by him, and the world knew him not. He came unto his own, and his own received him not. But as many as received him, to them gave he power to become the sons of God, even to them that believe on his name: Which were born, not of blood, nor of the will of the flesh, nor of the will of man, but of God. And the Word was made flesh, and dwelt among us, (and we beheld his glory, the glory as of the

only begotten of the Father,) full of
grace and truth. (John 1:1-14)

Even though we often see Christmas cards with
Jesus depicted as a baby with a halo shining above His
head; in the biblical account of the Christmas story, we
meet a little baby who didn't stand out from the crowd.
Herod had to ask the wise men to show him where to
find the child. When he realized that they had tricked
him, he had to kill all the babies in the region in an
attempt to execute the one he was looking for. Even
though there were supernatural events surrounding the
disclosure to the shepherds and the wise men, they
had to have explicit directions in order to find the Christ
child: the one wrapped in swaddling clothes and the
one in the house over which the star came to rest.

As we go through the life of Jesus, we see
repeatedly that He was indistinguishable from the
average man on the street. Even John the Baptist had
to ask if He were the one that all of Israel was looking
for. Judas had to kiss Him so the lynch mob would
know which man to arrest. In John 14:9 Jesus Himself
even turned to His followers and remarked, "Have I
been so long with you and you have not known Me?"
He even acknowledged that it took supernatural
intervention to get Peter to recognize Him as the Son of
God. These instances disclose to us that there must
be something wrong with the Jesus we see depicted in
the typical movie or Passion play. If Jesus were really
the blond-headed, blue-eyed girlish-looking character in
an otherwise dark-haired, dark-eyed manly cast, then it
would have been easy to pick Him out in any crowd.

The mystery of the incarnation is that Jesus could
blend into the mass of the human race and become as
indistinguishable as a needle in a haystack. But just as
a needle is not straw no matter how mingled it may

become in the hay, Jesus remained totally God even though He was totally enmeshed in humanity. He was still the High Priest even though He was touched with every feeling of infirmity common to man. Even though He was tempted by every sin we humans know, He was totally untainted by human sinfulness. Jesus came into the world as divinity in human flesh for a specific purpose and mission. Paul described this mission in Romans 8:3, "For what the law could not do, in that it was weak through the flesh, God sending his own Son in the likeness of sinful flesh, and for sin, condemned sin in the flesh." Peter summed it up in his sermon in Acts chapter four, "Neither is there salvation in any other: for there is none other name under heaven given among men, whereby we must be saved." John spelled it out in his first epistle, "For this purpose the Son of God was manifested, that he might destroy the works of the devil." Jesus Himself declared that the whole purpose for which He came into the world was to go to the cross. Yet during the Christmas season, it is so easy for us to get our attention on the little baby in the manger and to lose the incarnate God dwelling among men to redeem us from our sin. It is all too easy to lose the needle in the hay stacked in the manger. It is my prayer that this year, we don't miss the point of the incarnation -- Emanuel, God with us.

Who Put the "C" in "Christmas"?

In the only line I remember from the Christmas special of a long-forgotten sitcom, a Jewish lady who was trying to adjust to the Christian-dominated society made a statement about something which had to do with one of our holiday customs. Because Hanukah -- the Jewish holiday which roughly coincided with our Christmas -- is often spelled with a silent "C" at the front, she pronounced "Christmas" as if its initial "C" were also silent. When corrected, she replied, "'Hanukah,' 'Hristmas,' what's the difference?" The question inspires my question, "Who put the 'C' in 'Christmas,' anyway?"

The "C" in "Christmas" stands for curiosity -- the standard ingredient which has tormented each of us from the first time we eagerly waited to see what would magically appear under the tree to this very year when we still trying to guess what is in that one special package in its bright wrapping paper. Curiosity is the quality of Christmas which is so aptly described in the line of the popular song, "Every mother's child will find it hard to sleep tonight wondering if reindeer really know how to fly."

But where did curiosity come from? It was part of the very first Christmas when the shepherds suggested to one another, "Let's go see this thing that the angels are talking about." It was curiosity that led them to Bethlehem and to the baby Jesus! The shepherds put the "C" in "Christmas."

Well, if the "C" came from the shepherds, who put the "H" in "Christmas?" "H" is the element of hope which makes Christmas different from any of the other three hundred sixty-four days of the year. Christmas always seems to bring with it a new level of hope and expectation. We hope -- and really believe -- that we will hear from that long-lost friend or relative. We hope -- and actually dare to expect -- that there will be new relationships with those who have been distanced. We all have our Christmas wishes which we imagine will become reality -- no matter what the odds.

But where did hope come from? Hope became part of the story of the first Christmas when Simeon and Anna blessed the baby in the temple. The elderly twosome had served in the temple for years in the hope of seeing the Lord's messiah. Now, in the twilight years of their lives, the dreams and prayers which had been the burden of their hearts for decades were fulfilled before their age-dimmed eyes! To them, the whole message of Jesus' birth was a loud proclamation of hope! Anna and Simeon put the "H" in "Christmas."

Now, if it was Anna and Simeon who gave the "H," who provided the "R"? "R" stands for rejoicing -- the hallmark of the holiday. As if the whole world has been injected with "Joy to the World" to the point that the "city streetlights, even stoplights, flash a bright red and green," joy indelibly marks the season. From the music in the shopping mall to the carols of the church choirs to individuals whistling a tune as they go about their holiday chores to the general feeling which pervades the atmosphere -- rejoicing is the very thumbprint of the season.

But where did rejoicing come from? Rejoicing was birthed into the Nativity story when an angelic choir put on a private concert for a little band of shepherds on the Bethlehem hillside to announce tidings of great joy. It was the heavenly host who put the "R" in "Christmas."

Well, if we got the "R" from the celestial chorus, where did we get the "I"? The "I" stands for insight -- a quality of Christmas which may not be discussed as often as it is experienced. Although we seldom use the word, we could each testify to having had at least a little visit by the Ghost of Christmases Past, the Ghost of Christmas Present, and the Ghost of Christmases Yet to Come. Just like Ebenezer Scrooge, we can all point to something in the holiday season which has helped us to see our world from a new perspective.

But who introduced insight into the Christmas story? This job fell into the hands of the angel Gabriel who was sent from his comfortable heavenly quarters to the dusty little town of Nazareth to give a little virgin girl a new insight into God's overall plan for man: He was interested in man's needs and his condition, He could make a girl pregnant without her having human relationships, and He would use a little baby to save the human race. Next, Gabriel had to visit her boyfriend and give him a totally new insight into the scheme of things: God wanted him to bear the humility of a questionable marriage and share the dignity of raising the very Son of God. The angel Gabriel made insight a part of Christmas.

If it was from Gabriel that we got our "I," where did we get the "S"? The "S" stands for spirit -- the most obvious component of the holiday. In fact, the expression, "the Christmas spirit," enjoys universal usage. Even those who may not believe in God, accept the story of the virgin birth, or believe that the manger held the Incarnate Word of God willingly recognize that there is more than just merchandise and emotion involved. Even though they may call it the "magic of the season," they must admit that Christmas has its own unique synergy in which the holiday is far greater than the sum of its components of gift wrap, sleighs, men in red suits, and wooden camel cut-outs standing next to the manger scene on the front lawn of the church.

But how did the spirit become part of that first Christmas day? When the pregnant virgin visited her elderly cousin who was also supernaturally with child, Elizabeth's baby leapt inside her womb. The explanation was that the Holy Spirit had filled John the Baptist while still inside his mother's belly. Simply being in the presence of Jesus even though He was still inside Mary's womb was enough to activate a spiritual anointing upon the unborn prophet. Today, even though the real Jesus may be buried under a very thick façade of commercialism and myth, His presence -- right through the camouflage of contemporary society -- is enough to give a new sensation to the season. It was John the Baptist who brought the spirit to Christmas.

If it was John the Baptist who put the "S" in "Christmas," who was it who added the "T"? The "T" represents the treasures -- the stuff that the "shoppers rush home with" in that favorite seasonal song. The very theme of the holiday seems to be, "Gifts and presents for everyone," as we frantically count the shopping days until the Christmas deadline. The giving of gifts and exchanging of presents are such an integral part of the holiday that everyone in the retail business knows that he can always redeem himself from eleven months of poor performance with the sales of the one month leading up to Christmas.

We really don't have to ask how treasures became part of the original Christmas because we all instantly remember that the wise men trekked hundreds of miles for the privilege of presenting their treasures before the One who was born king of the Jews. It was the wise men who added the treasures to our holiday.

So, if it was the wise men who put the "T" in "Christmas," where did we get the "M"? The "M" represents memories -- a part of the holiday which no one could overlook. In fact, there is probably no other emotion which is more profound at this season than the power of memory, and there is probably no other season of the year which is more ripe with memories. We all have a full bank of memories associated with the holiday: memories of those magical mornings when, as children, we found those special surprises under the tree; reminiscences of Christmases past with those loved ones who are separated from us this present Christmas or who are no longer here to share any future Christmases; remembrances of Christmas milestones such as the first Christmas of your married life, the first Christmas in a new home or new city, baby's first Christmas, the first Christmas when the kids came back home after moving out of the house, and the first Christmas you had to share some of your family members with their spouses' families. Certainly, memory is part of the very fabric of Christmas.

But who introduced memory into the original Christmas recipe? It was the Mary who took all the events of that first Christmas and "pondered them in her heart" -- creating a store of memories for Christmases yet to come. It was the virgin Mary who gave us the "M."

If the virgin Mary brought us an "M" for Christmas, we must ask where did we get the "A"? This letter brings us to a part of Christmas which we would all love to skip; but without it, our word would not be complete. "A" stands for animosity -- the hard feelings which have been simmering against a sibling, another family member, an old girlfriend or boyfriend, or an ex-spouse. Unfortunately, it is all too often the case that it is only at holiday get-togethers that these latten conflicts are given occasion to vent. The crowded malls with long check-out lines and not enough parking spaces are also great breeding grounds for sudden flashes of animosity. You must certainly be asking why we are taking time to focus on such a negative facet of the holiday when there are so many happy aspects we could consider. The short answer is that the antagonistic feelings of the letter "A" are just as real as the warm, fuzzy memories represented by the letter "M."

But who brought animosity to that first Christmas morn? It was King Herod who showed up with a giant "A" in his heart and hand. When he tried to trick the wise men into leading him to the baby Jesus and when he decreed the Slaughter of the Innocents in his malicious attempt to destroy the Christ Child, King Herod infected our blessed holiday with the black plague of animosity. It was King Herod who put the "A" in Christmas."

If King Herod put the "A" in Christmas, who finished out the word by adding the "S"? This final installment represents savior -- the whole point of Christmas anyway.

> Behold, the angel of the Lord appeared
> unto him in a dream, saying, "Joseph,
> thou son of David, fear not to take unto
> thee Mary thy wife: for that which is
> conceived in her is of the Holy Ghost.
> And she shall bring forth a son, and
> thou shalt call his name JESUS: for he
> shall save his people from their sins."
> Now all this was done, that it might be
> fulfilled which was spoken of the Lord
> by the prophet, saying, "Behold, a

virgin shall be with child, and shall bring forth a son, and they shall call his name Emmanuel, which being interpreted is, God with us." Then Joseph being raised from sleep did as the angel of the Lord had bidden him, and took unto him his wife: And knew her not till she had brought forth her firstborn son: and he called his name JESUS. (Matthew 1:20-25)

And, lo, the angel of the Lord came upon them, and the glory of the Lord shone round about them: and they were sore afraid. And the angel said unto them, "Fear not: for, behold, I bring you good tidings of great joy, which shall be to all people. For unto you is born this day in the city of David a Saviour, which is Christ the Lord." (Luke 2:9-11)

It was Jesus who put the salvation in Christmas!!!

Christmas at the
Roof Top of the World

Nestled along the Himalayan Mountains among the highest peaks in the world is a tiny isolated Hindu nation where until very recently the populace revered their king more as a living god than as their human ruler. Until just a few years ago, Christmas was forbidden in this nation at the roof top of the world -- witnessing to the citizens of the country, converting to Christianity, and even owning Bibles were offenses punishable by imprisonment and torture. It was in this far-flung nation the Lord answered my prayer from the Where's Waldo? chapter in this book. It was in the towering Himalayas that I was commissioned to "go tell it on the mountains that Jesus Christ is born!" He not only granted me the desire of my heart, but He did it on the grandest scale possible -- He broke through centuries of Nepal's isolation so that I could freely proclaim from the highest mountains in the world the Christmas message that Jesus Christ is born.

It all began in 1986 when I was challenged to pray for the nation of Nepal which was totally closed to the gospel at that time. In my prayers every day for the next four years, I claimed Proverbs 21:1 that the Lord would turn the king's heart. Finally, the news came that a new political freedom had been granted and that now total religious liberty was permitted to the people. Soon afterwards, the Lord opened the doors for me to visit Nepal to do short-term mission work; since that time, I have returned each year and have been given an entrance into the hearts of the people of the nation. Pastors' conferences, tract distribution, church ministry, and publishing of books in the Nepali language are all part of the ministry that the Lord granted to my wife and me in this far-flung kingdom. Yet, there is one very special part of our work that is always a highlight of our trip.

This special event is our visit at the Mendies Haven Home for Children in Kathmandu, a privately-operated orphanage founded by a Canadian lady, lovingly known as "Mommie Mendies." In many ways, Mommie reminded us of Mother Teresa -- and quite naturally so, since the two ladies became close friends from the day that Mrs. Mendies first began her work with the children of Calcutta prior to her eventual relocation in Nepal where she gave more than fifty years to providing a home, an education, and a future to the otherwise hopeless children of this third-world nation.

With no organization or major sponsors to support it, the Mendies Haven relies totally upon the gifts from friends such as us to help provide for the children. Each year we get to bring "Christmas" to the roof top of the world as we share with the children the clothes, shoes, school supplies, candies, and toys which we have brought for them. In trying to describe the reaction of these precious children I can only say that they simply do not have enough face to hold all the smiles! In addition, we slip several boxes away for safe keeping in a closet for the several months until the actual Christmas Day! One year as we were selecting the gifts to bring, we felt directed to buy a volleyball set. Packing and transporting the poles was going to be a real challenge, so I really hesitated to make the purchase. Finally, I denied my head and followed my heart to buy the playground set. When we arrived at the orphanage, we were greeted with the news that -- only two hours before -- they had just finalized the negotiations to purchase the field next door to be used as a playground for the children. One of the top priorities on this new plot of land would be to build a volley ball court. You can imagine how we all celebrated Christmas when the children unwrapped our big package!

Wise Men Still Seek Him

I want to share with you a few closing thoughts about the birth of Christ. Although these thoughts are centered around the Christmas story, the complete message has as much to do with Christ's second coming as with His first. We are all aware that most of the people who saw Jesus come and live and die still did not realize who He was. Simply put, they missed Him! Now that it is about time for Him to come back, we need to take a look at the people who didn't miss Him. We need to pattern our lives after them. We need to find their secret!

Let's start at a rather odd place for a Christmas story -- Daniel chapter nine. Here we read about Daniel, who had seen visions, interpreted dreams, and done great acts of the Lord. In this passage, he says that he perceived from books that the Lord would deliver Israel after seventy years in exile. The Lord had stated this very plainly in Jeremiah 25:11-12 and 29:10, but Daniel had not seen it the first time he had read the prophet's book. Yet, praise God, this time he found the key! As he prayed and fasted over the revelation, God spoke to him. (Daniel 9:24) After sixty-nine weeks of years, or four hundred eighty-three years, the messiah would come. Jewish history rushed toward that prophetic year.

As the Star of Bethlehem shone and as angels sang, most of Israel must have been aware that it was time for their messiah to come. In fact, many false leaders rose up and claimed to be the messiah. Acts 5:36-37 and 21:38 mention some of them, and history books point out even more. Many of the people were deceived. Does that sound similar to our situation today? With so many teachings, ideas, and doctrines -

- how will we know what to believe? Let's take a look at the Christmas story and see how the people there knew which messiah to follow.

First, let's look at Mary. The Lord showed her personally through an angel. (Luke 1:26-35) But what about Joseph? Being betroth to Joseph, Mary must have told him about her visit from the angel and about the son she would bare through the Holy Spirit. However, when the promise began to come true, Joseph had to have a personal word from God before he could understand. (Matthew 1:18-25) The Lord also confirmed it to the priest Zechariah through an angel. In the same way, He called the shepherds to the manger. The wise men, as you remember, were beckoned to the nativity by a star; they were warned against Herod in a dream. But Simeon and Anna, in the temple at Jerusalem, received the word that Jesus was the Christ directly from the Holy Spirit. (Luke 2:21-28)

Now what about us? Should we wait for an angel or a great sign to herald Christ's second coming? No! Revelation 16:14 warns us about watching for signs -- in the last days, demons will have a great power to fool those who are looking for signs. Jesus Himself warned us not to follow signs, "Then if any man shall say unto you, Lo, here is Christ, or there; believe it not. For there shall arise false Christs, and false prophets, and shall shew great signs and wonders; insomuch that, if it were possible, they shall deceive the very elect. Behold, I have told you before. Wherefore if they shall say unto you, Behold, he is in the desert; go not forth: behold, he is in the secret chambers; believe it not." (Matthew 24:23-26)

Instead of seeking for signs, we need to be like Simeon the priest and Anna the prophetess. They were servants of the Lord who had dedicated their lives to the study of the Word, prayer, and fasting. Simeon was "righteous and devout, looking for the consolation of Israel, and the Holy Spirit was upon him." He had been told by the Spirit that he would not die until he had seen the Christ. Imagine how his heart must have pounded each time one of the self-proclaimed messiahs came to Jerusalem. He must have looked at each one with great hope -- but each time the Spirit spoke to his heart and said, "No, this is not the one. Wait. He is still coming." Then came that day when a little baby boy was placed in the old priest's arms. Just a little eight-day-old boy; far from the great leaders Simeon had seen marching in Jerusalem; just a little back-woods carpenter's son -- but THE TRUE MESSIAH! Hallelujah! The old priest's heart really pounded this time! The Spirit of God witnessed that this was the "light to lighten the Gentiles and the glory of thy people Israel."

Simeon's revelation of Christ came from the Holy Spirit. This is the same Holy Spirit that reveals Christ to us even today. The key is listening when the Spirit speaks! Simeon was prepared for Christ's first coming because of his dynamic relationship with the Holy Spirit. In the same way, our charismatic life in the Spirit should prepare us for His second coming. Jesus stated that the Holy Spirit would "take what is mine and declare it to you." (John 16:14) As we live each day deeper and deeper in the Holy Spirit, we will have more and more revelation of Christ. Thus, our lives in the Spirit will prepare us to see Him on the day of His manifestation. Praise God! Let's be Simeons and listen when the Spirit speaks to us at Christmas -- and at any other season of the year.

CPSIA information can be obtained
at www.ICGtesting.com
Printed in the USA
FSOW02n1605011215
13789FS

9 780982 767832